THE NEW YORK TIMES
BOOK OF VERSE

The New York Times
BOOK OF VERSE

Edited by Thomas Lask

A NEW YORK TIMES BOOK

The Macmillan Company, New York, N.Y.
Collier-Macmillan Ltd., London

All poems in this volume originally appeared in *The New York Times*.
Unless otherwise indicated, copyrights are held by the individual poets
or their estates and all rights are reserved. Grateful acknowledgment
is made for permission to reprint them in this volume.

"The Adamant" and "The Bat" appeared in *The Collected Poems of
Theodore Roethke*, copyright 1938 by Theodore Roethke. Reprinted
by permission of Doubleday & Company, Inc.

"Incident With Lions" and "Portrait of A Certain Gentleman" appeared
in *A Footing On This Earth*, copyright 1961 by Sara Henderson Hay.
Reprinted by permission of Doubleday & Company, Inc.

"Shiva" appeared in *Selected Poetry of Robinson Jeffers*, copyright
1938 by Robinson Jeffers. Reprinted by permission of Random House,
Inc.

"Little Dreams" appeared in *Little Dreams*, by Langston Hughes. Re-
printed by permission of *The New York Times* and Harold Ober
Associates, Inc.

"A Blade of Grass," by Oscar Williams, is reprinted by permission of
the executors of the Estate of Oscar Williams.

"The Manzanita," by Yvor Winters, appeared in *The Giant Weapon*,
copyright 1943 by New Directions. Reprinted by permission of New
Directions Publishing Corporation.

"Fiftieth Birthday" appeared in *New And Selected Poems*, copyright
1967 by Peter Viereck, published by Bobbs-Merrill Co. Reprinted by
permission of Peter Viereck.

"Polemic" appeared in *Imperatives*, copyright 1962 by Anthony Ostroff.
Reprinted by permission of Harcourt Brace Jovanovich, Inc.

"The Lace Maker" appeared in *Looking Up At Leaves*, copyright 1966

"What Is Unwoven" appeared in *Estrangements*, by Arthur Freeman. Reprinted by permission of Harcourt Brace Jovanovich, Inc.
"A Prayer for His Lady," by Oliver St. John Gogarty, reprinted by permission of The Devin-Adair Company.
"The Wise Child" appeared in *Confessions and Histories*, by Edward Lucie-Smith. Reprinted by permission of Oxford University Press.

ACKNOWLEDGMENTS

It is a pleasure to acknowledge the help of a number of people who made the book possible:

Lee Foster, whose idea it was; John Stewart who made the idea flesh; Arthur Gregor, my editor at Macmillan, whose patience with and quiet resolution of my problems always made me wonder later why I had been so troubled.

Mary Campanelli worked with me on every stage in the preparation of the book. Only she and I know how great her contribution was.

Finally I wish to thank Charles Merz, former editor of the editorial page of *The New York Times*, and John B. Oakes, the current editor, both of whom felt that there was a place for poetry on the page and who, though sometimes puzzled by the choices, found room for them.

CONTENTS

EDITOR'S PREFACE

THE POEMS IN THIS BOOK are a selection of the poetry printed on the editorial page of *The New York Times* over the last fifty years. They are not chronological, however; and though they have been grouped together under various subject headings, they were not chosen to illustrate them. That is, the poems were not picked as samples of love poems or nature poems or poems of death and dissolution and the like.

The aim of the book is simply to provide a body of work that will be a pleasure to read and, we hope, one that the reader will want to return to. And though many of these poems have appeared in the poets' own books of verse, we wanted to salvage what we could from the transitory nature of newspaper publication.

Some of the names will be familiar to all readers of poetry; some will be more familiar to readers of the editorial page. Some will not be familiar at all, since *The Times* has always been receptive to poetry that is occasionally written by men and women whose major interests lie elsewhere. It has been this editor's experience that in times of great emotional tension or upheaval (as in the assassination of President John F. Kennedy or the landing on the moon), unnumbered people, who would not normally use verse forms at all, try to express their feelings in poetry. As with nations so with individuals. Occasionally a man writing out of strong feeling may manage a nicely turned poem based on his experience.

Though generally contemporary in tone, texture, and outlook, the poems are not violently experimental. There is good reason for this. It is not that *The Times* is against the avant-garde. It is simply that it doesn't think a newspaper column is the place for such work. The average reader would only be put off by what he would consider extremism. It is a fact of life that the man who can work his way through American foreign policy in Africa or the merits of the oil depletion allowances or who may even be an expert of sorts on local birds is not necessarily one who understands or is at home in modern verse. Nothing would be gained by publishing the "Maximus" poems of Charles Olson or the "Owlwise by Altarlight" poems of Dylan Thomas. Nor, because of the nature of newspaper columns, would it be wise to run chunks from long sequences of poems or poems that demand odd or sometimes bizarre settings. Tricky type setting in the hurley-burley of putting out a daily newspaper can be a dangerous thing.

On the other hand, *The Times* has moved away from pastel-colored, tradition-anchored nature verse or poems expressing predictable sentiments on pious subjects like mother or dogs. It has tried to make the poems relevant to our times. There is nothing more dismaying than to find on an editorial page that deals with the most contemporary of material, poems that would have been old-fashioned a century ago. Relevancy, however, does not mean that the poems have to gloss the day's news. In fact *The Times* has tried to avoid printing poems that are tied too closely to the news. But we hope that the poems will show the relevancy by their forms, by their contemporary feel and outlook, in their use of language and subject matter.

Recently, after a reading in New York, a Czech poet in exile, who was asked about technical innovations in Czechoslovakia, answered that young people were turning more and more to free verse. This did not seem much of an innovation to some in the audience. But the poet pointed out Czech poetry had been so dominated by Russian verse and its symmetrical forms that the turn to free verse represented something of a revolution.

We hope that these poems will reflect their own generation and yet have enough merit and quality to appeal to future ones.

THOMAS LASK

THE NEW YORK TIMES
BOOK OF VERSE

PART I

THE COURSE OF LOVE

Contract

The hall clock, metal teethed to metal,
whirs its wheels to keep
sixteen chimes before the hour
that tolls itself to sleep.

I heard the clock when summer wind
creaked branches, heard the slow
addition of its muffled chime.
Now overhead the snow

shifts, swirls on shingles; and the sound
of metal shrunk with cold
strikes with a clearer, harder voice
than summer's. Why hands fold

into each other to be one
is a mystery the house
speaks to itself, board on beam,
and beam to board laid close.

And why a heart in cold contract
with itself can break beyond
the blindness spoken by the hands
of lovers is my bond

kept with the metal, learned from clocks
chiming the night away;
while two together locking hands
must whisper: "Stay. Stay, stay."

FREDERICK NICKLAUS

"I Could Take"

I could take
two leaves
   and give you one.
Would that not be
a kind of perfection?

But I prefer
One leaf
   torn to give you half showing

(after these years, simply)
love's complexity in an act,
   the tearing and the unique edges—

one leaf (one word) from the two
imperfections that match.

HAYDEN CARRUTH

Pinwheel

I fear one minute more than twenty years.
In twenty years, my darling, you and I
may grow to fit our futures. We may die
or part, or learn forbearance. Today's fears
cause me to clap my hands against my ears.
This coming moment screeches from our sky
harsh as a bomb. Flung on my face I lie
tense, till the rowdy rumor of it clears.

The past is peace and quiet, or at most
dreams in a sleep. Far future is a risk
not yet to take. All time's a harmless ghost
except this minute, pressing harsh and brisk
on to the next, spun like a croupier's disk,
with all our kindness to be won or lost.

DILYS LAING

To Mary, of Sailing

My moods are as a sailboat coming through
Your eye of wind: an ease of coasting calm
Between our energies, an avenue
Dividing action, when across my palm
The sheets lie loose and light as our long love,
Then harden up to blocks and slatting sail,
Go taut, all silent but the hum above
Of rigging and the hiss of leeward rail;
So to your freshening caprice I heel
And by your spirit come alive and trim,
Yet parry too your puffs which threaten keel
And capsize in their sudden interim.
Then do our balanced buoyancies embrace:
My lane of wake upon your cat's paw grace.

RICHARD SNYDER

Penelope

Under the lime tree
I pause from my ravelling
to garden you like
an imaginary flower,
bending your absent mind,
heliotropic,
toward my sun.
When I bathe,
naked as a pebble
in the weedy pool,
the black rippling wake
intrudes your sleep
with a caress.
I am the exile.
Your olive child
lays his head across
my thighs, and I
sigh after the wind,
groping through the cleft
between the hills
to find the sea.

JUDY THURMAN

Portrait in Stone

(For H. G.)

Face in stone and
Stone in face:
Compacted in this still embrace
Neither displaces either.

The eye that married them,
Grown wiser with the deed,
A twofold matrimony thus
Makes mind and eye unanimous.

The labyrinth of strokes
Has left the rockheart sheer,
That eye and mind may taste the calm
(Want and discord found it there)

And, with their satisfaction, know
The strength that bred this radiance
And brimmed the surface of the stone
To rule a city with a glance.

CHARLES TOMLINSON

Absence

The distance widens
though I do not move.
The room becomes a hall
the hall an acre
rimmed by trees; the trees
fall back to water
and I cannot reach to one of these.

This is the place
love leads me to
without caves or corners
where land is measureless
as air and shadows without bone
fly above the straw
where under a wide and faceless sky
I am clutched by absence
as by a claw.

JEAN BURDEN

What Is Unwoven

Never, though sky from sky divide by night,
and sea, beneath the prow, relinquish sea,
though star with starfall part, and perish light,
never so casually shall we.

Nor though the senseless particles of stone
diversify to dust, and rest apart,
and frailty corrupting flesh and bone
dissolve all but the heart.

Though dark chagrin accumulate like tears,
and bitterness like wind behind the sky,
though reason lift the mist, and tell our years,
we shall not wholly comply.

Yet we shall part; we know it, and know why.
As every element knows bliss and bane,
we know our pain and pleasure; as the sky
divides by gentlest rain

We shall divide. Dearest, but as the sea
makes one once more behind the parting prow,
memory, like a wake, must bind and weave
what is unwoven now.

ARTHUR FREEMAN

Poem

Something, so great a sweetness, came
With your blithe, gentled, hale and golden
Gayness: a mirth as of a changeling's, yet
Silken-sheathed with true love's kindness;
A self-sufficing, airy, free
Witty and dulcet gallantry
That haunts me like a summer I surprised
Upon some docile lawn ringed white with daisies
And clouds that past the lily go
In their sumptuousness of snow
And ah, that scent
Of roses faint with heat
That breathed, I thought,
Your incarnations out.

JEAN GARRIGUE

A Prayer for His Lady

If it be kindness, God, be kind
To her tall fragrant form and mind
And leave her in this world of ours
Unageing as she is in Yours;
And let not Time's contagion blur
The image of Your dream in her.

Little enough we have we know
Of Love in Life to lead us through,
And Loveliness is on the wing:
Leave the wild cherry to the Spring
In spangling showers to tremble away;
But for Your grace preserve the clay.

OLIVER ST. J. GOGARTY

Somewhere in Tuscany

Somewhere in Tuscany, in April, beyond Pisa:
A hillock beneath a castle, off the road,
There was a little canal at the foot, and hay plots
Where our daughter cried out with delight at a slick green
    lizard.
Then a steep path, under fruit trees barely in bud,
A bank near a standpipe tap, a place for our stove to bubble,
For the children to slice fresh bread, and lay out the sheep-
    cheese, and butter—
A scramble of paper, tin plates, and browned veal medallions
Tormenting our road-glum mouths. Then the wine, the wine!
The sparkling pale local white wine with its bitter touch!
Oh, but nothing—a scratch family picnic, on some nameless
    battlement mound,
A string of passing children, singing like angels, lugging babies,
Two lovers who paused at a faucet to splash their faces,
"Buon giornos" from passersby, as if we belonged to their
    village.
Nothing! Yet such a sun-relaxed moment.
I am sitting there still, as September begins to strip us,
So familiar, the stony soil, the orchard, the vine terraces!
Such greetings as made us belong—yet to nowhere, just a
    corner
Where we sat sipping white Chianti, and, as we knelt in the
    rain-touched dust,
My love for you flashed like the lizard, among the crusts.

DAVID HOLBROOK

A Quality of Pain

There is a quality of pain
That burnishes the heart
As if the finest jewelers' rouge
That brings the metal out
By blending every scratch and stain
Were rubbed against one place
The way a woman polishes
Away her bitterness.

Love is an abrasive.
Its touch we dare endure
Who give our dowries outright
And acquiesce to bear
A quiet splendor left to us
When all the scars are fused:
The patina the heart acquires
Only from being used.

BARBARA D. HOLENDER

A Game of Cards

Determined to be peaceful, we played cards,
Dealt out the hands and hid from one another
Our power. Our only words were weightless words
Like "Your turn," "Thank you"—words to soothe and
    smother;
Our pulses, slowed to softness, moved together.
So we became opponents and could stare
Like strangers, guessing what the other held.
There was no look of love or passion there.
The pasteboard figures sheltered us, compelled
Each one to win. Love was another world.
And yet within the concentration which
Held us so fast, some tenderness slipped in,
Some subtle feeling which could deftly breach
The kings and queens and prove the pasteboard thin:
Another battle thundered to begin.

ELIZABETH JENNINGS

Song

As if from the Spanish

Because he was gone, without a goodbye
But with his guitar, that trap and cage of hearts,
She sat on a stone on the crest of the hill,
Grieving that love arrives, that love departs.
Adiós, she said, Go away, Mr. Blackbird,
I have no mind to watch you flutter and dart . . .
To which the blackbird uttered a dirty
Word from out of his black heart.
Adiós, she said, Go away, Mr. Lizard,
I have no heart to watch you scuttle and dote . . .
To which the lizard uttered a dark
Remark from out of his pallid throat.
Adiós, she said . . . But I am a liar!
Stiffened to silence by the dismay
Of lost love, she sat on that stone,
Looked once at each and at me, and looked away.

LYSANDER KEMP

Puzzle

All things find their road. The bee its hive,
The bat its cavern, every lark its nest;
All things that walk or crawl or swim or dive
Clear for the right road when it's time to rest.
The gull will trail a thousand leagues to sea,
And foxes trail a week's run from their brood;
And one at last will veer back to its quay,
The others turn back to their patch of wood.
All things must find their road. The mouse its mead,
The ant its hillock, every seed its loam;
No matter where the vagrant highways lead,
The heart cannot forget its way back home.

Why then must my senses fret and stir
With fear I've lost the road that leads to her?

SIDNEY COOKSLEY

Twin Epitaph

My Love:
Good, the earth gathered us into one garland.
Ours is the truest kiss, with lips of stone.
The longer the night, the nearer the wonderland.
Death has seven wonders, life none.

MENKE KATZ

Sarcophagus Cover

This handsome pair,
All mortal sharing done,
Rest in each other's arms,
Bound by a common shroud.

The gossamer gravecloth
Sculptured in supple bas-relief,
Purls like a shallow stream around
The stonefixed sleepers.

Not like the chapelled pairs
That keep their decorous sleep
In rigid parallel, hands pointing
Heavenward, renouncing touch.

The woman holds her lover close
As though to bend his head down
For her kiss. His arm
Guards her. In the stone box,

Bones and dust mingle.
The lovers who pause here,
Hands tight-locked, hearts chilled
At the thought of final sundering,
Envy these effigies.

RUTH FELDMAN

Waking

She is so young, becoming a stranger.
Knowing something of her body's moods,
she feels the imprecision of what moves
within herself, where none can reassure her.

Her sleep was comfortable and sure.
Waking is a strange world, not her own,
and who she was will not survive the room
she wakes in, which no longer knows her.

Feeling her body gather from its sleep
she turns and stretches, stands and pads
across the dark floor, lifts the shade . . .
all light pours sensuous and steep.

All light will hold her. Its form
is her flesh, where she holds the light
or lacks it. If once she was transparent,
now she shapes it. Its shape to her is warm.

Shape is feeling then: how her body wakes
and is unsure, how it is undisciplined
from long sleep, and will not be defined
in any shape except the light it breaks.

JON ANDERSON

Irregular Sonnet for a Marriage

You know you'll play the wedding theme
for this girl too: pairs of turtledoves,
many kinds of blessings. Crows' feet and love's
yellow teeth have no place in this scheme

of innocence and new mirrors.
Bless the groom, then kiss the bride.
Don't forget the little one that stirs
between her and the man's one pride.

Forget now the quicksilver blotches, the margin
of half-eyes, the wink of the ex-virgin.
If black and purple carrier-pigeons

flutter from places in her unwed past,
just wring their necks.

        You'll like the taste
when you find you too can lay a ghost.

A. K. RAMANUJAN

For Karen

What do you carry that cannot be borne,
That even in your most graceful risings
Your balance must waver, as now you stride
Over thresholds, though your boyishness betrays,
The long heels threaten to spill you forward,
Though your hard sweet bones must soften to let life in?

Your true burdens are what I cannot see,
Nothing like rock, nothing like bits of sky,
Rather, a heaviness of gifts and favors,
Until another season brings your beauty whole:
A woman, the future set calmly on her head,
Like a figure poised homeward from a well.

And yet you tottered when you rose—
Only as the inmost leaf tips toward light,
Only as the brightest pool echoes shade—
Yet tottered, and smiled, and stood. I say it outright:
It cannot be borne; the weight of life is cruel,
Though you step like a dancer from this room.

DANIEL HUGHES

THE STRIVING

The Adamant

Thought does not crush to stone.
The great sledge drops in vain.
Truth never is undone;
Its shafts remain.

The teeth of knitted gears
Turn slowly through the night,
But the true substance bears
The hammer's weight.

Compression cannot break
A center so congealed.
The tool can chip no flake:
The core lies sealed.

THEODORE ROETHKE

To Helen

(After Valery)

O Sea! . . . 'Tis I, risen from death once more
To hear the waves' harmonious roar
And see the galleys, sharp, in dawn's great awe
Raised from the dark by the rising and gold oar.

My fickle hands sufficed to summon kings
Their salt beards amused my fingers, deft and pure.
I wept. They sang of triumphs now obscure:
And the first abyss flooded the hull as if with falling wings.

I hear the profound horns and trumpets of war
Matching the rhythm, swinging of the flying oars:
The galleys' chant enchains the foam of sound;
And the gods, exalted at the heroic prow,
E'en though the spit of spray insults each smiling brow,
Beckon to me with arms indulgent,
    frozen, sculptured,
      and dead long long ago.

DELMORE SCHWARTZ

For the Antigone

No Socrates to teach her a last love,
Not even autumn. I seem to recall some lilacs,
The crispness of the road and the frost just broken,
A fine morning for March. I am pretty sure of the place
But perhaps it all happened at some different time;
You know what havoc memory plays with an old man.
She lay, and her neck was broken.
There was a kind of darkness hung about her,
As if the shadows to which she had kept faith
Had loved her and made her body fruitful. And even if
I saw the accidental blue of the choked veins,
I saw death and it flourished. Her presence
Seemed hypocritical. Most of us thought her small
And not so beautiful; I mean before these things.
Worn with the cares of keeping a large house
And courted by much death, her end was not
Entirely unexpected. Yet there was
A kind of devotion in her, life and law.
Say that these words will not appease the dead
Or force them to remain at what natural places
We have assigned to them. Or say that I am afraid,
It may well be. The sin is to forget.
A streak of blood had dried in her left ear,
Her body was a field of asphodels.

ANDRAS HAMORI

Variations on Simonides

Stranger, tell the Spartans we lie here,
Obedient to the rigorous Spartan star.
Traveler, tell them how the gates were passed,
Through traitors, not through us who fought and lost.
Stranger, say we kept the iron gain
Of the black broth of comrades and of men.
Do not say we thought we gave our breath
To save the repressive country of our youth.
Report, as we were bade, we made our end,
Not dreaming that all Hellas was our land.
We combed our hair and raised our swords to die.
We left our sons to flesh a further day.
Hot gates froze shut the sequences of time:
We bleed in a laconic epigram.
A narrow country narrowly defines.
We did our narrow best in narrow lines.

GLADYS ELY

Snow in the Caucasus

Snow in the Caucasus! Feather on feather
Fall softly and cover
Sonia's rooftree, the camp of her lover.
Come swiftly, white weather!

Blot out the roads! Take the ungarnered grain!
Be a trap of cold steel!
Fasten your teeth in the foreigner's heel.
Be fox-fire in his brain.

Transform his maps into glittering fable
Enticing his horde.
Smooth each ravine as a linen-clad board—
Oh, prepare him a table!

Bred of your bone, we have drowsed in your keeping
The long Winters through. . . .
With life to be gained, or the dying to do,
The Bear is not sleeping.

YETZA GILLESPIE

The War Museum at Nagasaki

Here are two helmets, stamped
With the marks of burning death,
A twisted toy in a case,
Its glass smoked by the breath
Of a passerby;
Dim in the photograph
A dying patient's face
Smiling patiently;
Where the moment tramped
He holds a bitter staff.

A woman pauses now,
Fixing her face in the glass,
Squinting to read the words
That summon up the crass
Immoment, silly facts:
The dates of birth and dying,
Name, height, the broken sherds
Of long-dead artefacts;
Broken is that bough;
The rest is useless lying.

Our pity, their regret
Are lost before the fact
Of truth, the hollow howl,
The twisted, worthless trace
Of broken wedding-rings.

Nothing, nothing can work,
Not love nor sorrow, yet,
One registers those things,
Throwing the dead a net
Across that foundering dark.

CHARLES HIGHAM

The Parachutes

Nothing can turn them from the ends that call.
Battalion on battalion, soldiers fall
Where no resistance is, their motions sure
Though distance and the sunlight make them blur.
So random mass and certain motion blend
In each specific flight and anguished end.
Though each conforms to law, no man can guess
Unique trajectories through nothingness.
Their undulations through unaltering blue
Mark but their passages, yet they are true:
True line and arc, pure drift and sudden flare,
Forms that contain the emptiness of air.
The sterile blossoms, empty clouds of thread,
Configurations of the utter dead,
Fall from the wastes; then, terror without sound,
Collapse in lethal petals on the ground.

CHARLES GULLANS

On Luck

The lucky live like Oedipus,
Without luck. No fuss, no fate;
They string along, tenacious, late.
Their sockets scorn the light where darkness
Towers eternally toward the sun.
They find themselves against the wall.
Like Humpty Dumpty how they fall!
Achilles, Hector, how they run!

MARK GOLDMAN

Incident with Lions

Into the Ark, by docile two and seven,
The obedient animals filed.
But there were some, I think, too proud, too wild
Thus to be herded and driven.
Lions, surely, who shook the night with thunder
There on the last hill,
Drenched and bedraggled and doomed, but imperial still,
Watching the world go under.
Noah had trouble finding some of that kin
Whom he could hustle aboard.
At bay, the princely lions paced and roared
And would not save their skin.
They stood while the heavens split and the flood rolled
And chose to drown deep
To the company of jackal and rat and the witless sheep
In the Ark's stinking hold.

SARA HENDERSON HAY

Charley III

(DMZ, Sept. 7, 1967)

No more the wide Mawnkato pearled with ice under blue
                                        January sky
your glad arm around the shoulder of the friend who ran faster
no more the long hours pad in hand composing reasons for
                                        your belief
a belief in fathers has no reason

no more the simple passion of going first
your hatless straightness, the struggle, the deep worry, the dark
                                        Africa of being alive in a
                                        country run by chiefs
                                        without tribes
no more of all that, only your brief beauty in many hearts
in a time when fathers bury their sons, and you surrounded,
                                        cut down
in a war you were fated never to see, blinded by love for all
                                        men.

STEPHEN SANDY

Cablegram

If Merlin did not lie, come quickly, King!
as once you came when crumbling realms appealed.
Surely, by now, your ancient wounds have healed.
After long sleep, you must be listening.

Within our gate the vultures sit and sing.
Return, and let the barren battlefield
bloom with your standards! Lend the weak your shield,
and let your great axe through the wildwood ring!

Say but the word; our lips have need to vow.
Say but the word; our eyes desire to blaze.
See how beneath your sacred sword we bow!
Oh send us shining through the world's dark ways!
So many battles, King, till you be gone
once more, in grief and blood, to Avalon . . .

AARON KRAMER

"Peace Was My Earliest Love"

Peace was my earliest love, and I presume
Will be my latest; but today, adult,
Arguing not to prove but for result
Opposing concepts in this thoughtful room,
I wonder at whose prompting, schooled by whom
I urged that Peace the Slogan, Peace the Cult,
Could turn the edge of sledge and catapult
And leave us calm to cull the grafted bloom.

In all my life I never knew a thing
So highly prized to be so cheaply had:
Longing to wed with Peace, what did we do?—
Sketched her a fortress on a paper pad;
Under her casement twanged a lovesick string;
Left wide the gate that let her foeman through.

EDNA ST. VINCENT MILLAY

Elegy

O fortunate man! who tilled the stubborn soil
Of hearts, undeviant from your earliest vow—
With what deep silence we review your toil,
Your hope . . . a parable now.

ARTHUR DAVISON FICKE

Shiva

There is a hawk that is picking the birds out of our sky.
She killed the pigeons of peace and security.
She has taken honesty and confidence from nations and men,
She is hunting the lonely heron of liberty.
She loads the arts with nonsense, she is very cunning,
Science with dreams and the state with powers to catch them
    at last.
Nothing will escape her at last, flying nor running
This is the hawk that picks out the stars' eyes.
This is the only hunter that will ever catch the wild swan.
The prey she will take last is the wild white swan of the
    beauty of things.
Then she will be alone, pure destruction, achieved and
    supreme.
Empty darkness under the death-tent wings.
She will build a nest of the swan's bones and hatch a new
    brood,
Hang new heavens with new birds, all be renewed.

ROBINSON JEFFERS

Watson and the Shark

Among the Stuart heads
and Copley furbelows
that fish ate up my youth.

Stretched in a jellied sea,
nude torso up, his eyes
cast backwards into pearls,
and dragging a fibrous stump
that belched brown smoke, that sailor
lay, while his shipmates groped
above for the upflung hand,
or poised long spears and oars
to fend those onrushing teeth.

But however long I stared,
shifting from foot to foot,
or lay awake wide-eyed
after the dream, that fish won.

The child's in league with truth.

He has been there since then,
in whatever white-frothed lane
of the sea, shearing the limbs
of hope and sailing-men;
and all our downcast eyes,
our cutting spears and oars
cannot beat into that hide
one hint—of how it feels
to be severed piece from piece.

PAUL PETRIE

Crime Story

They say that when a murder victim dies
A face is fixed forever in his eyes;
The colors never run, the image still
Looms through the retina its bleak surmise.

It is a tale. The other night I rose
And walked a beach, and saw the seagulls close
Tonged claws upon the carrion they killed.
Two lovers there embracing, I suppose,

Or rocks humped high to trick the wandering brain;
So may those nets, those masts, that gutted wain
Have seemed, not been; so the stretched limbs, the shrill
Cry of that dying seaman in his pain.

His lids were closed. It seemed no gaze was left.
Yet when I looked into the warp and weft
Of veins, I saw no image of a will
That someone drove upon him in the cleft

Under that rock's dead brow. Only a gleam
As though he'd smiled when, waking from a dream,
He saw the arm strike downward; the blood spill
Coldly upon a splintered mizzenbeam.

I think whoever slew him filled a need,
Plumped some dark hollow, satisfied a greed,
And rode away. I cannot know it till
I meet her, riding lifeward on her steed.

CHARLES HIGHAM

· 38 ·

End of a Fairy Tale

as not told to the children

He was, of course, the first
of four and twenty to survive
the wood's ordeal.
Creeper-throttled and thorn-pierced,
three and twenty princes swung behind
rotting each in a golden rind.
He gave God thanks: but to arrive
was not the miracle.
What brought him to his armoured knees,
for the first time, in the tower
was finding, at an hour
when petals through the palace's garden close,
unfolding, at his touch, the Rose.

JON STALLWORTHY

After the Record Is Broken

My mind slips back to lesser men,
Their how, their when.
Champions then:
Big Stilley, with his bandaged hands,
Broke through the Sidney line, the stands
Hysterical, profuse the rival bands.
Poor Ackerman, his spikes undone,
His strap awry, gave way to none,
Not even pride. The mile he won.

How higher, faster, farther. Stars crossed
Recede, and legends twinkle out, far lost,
Far discus-spun and javelin-tossed,
Nor raise again that pull and sweat,
That dig and burn, that crouch-get-set
Aglimmer in old trophies yet.
Now smoother, softer, trimmed for speed,
The champion seems a better breed,
His victory a showroom deed.

Oh, what have we to do with men
Like champions, but cry again
How high, how fast, how far? What then?
Remember men when records fall.
Unclap your hands, draw close your shawl:
The lesser men have done it all.

JAMES A. EMANUEL

Discobolus

tensed
beneath a shaft
of action
bent
in parentheses
heavier
than an arm

discus
is held
to a throw
beyond
a laurel wreath

breaking
a former record
he bends
and waits

for a second coming
halfway
between windup
and sprung

(question)
mark along
a trajectory
traced
against Iowa sun

DAVID A. LOCHER

Homage to Aesop

How the body burns and races
Cleanly past the plod of mind
That blunders up the road, and traces
Mocking dust a mile behind

How the vivid body heaves
Quicksilver pawprints toward a prize
It counts as won, while startled leaves
And grasses lift astonished eyes

But mind, beneath its stony shell
Of delicacy, half-afraid
Shyly celebrates the pebbles,
Petals, ferns and stripes of shade

When the body, burnt with burning
Spends its gleaming heat in haste,
Mind comes, laboring at learning
Matter. Silver speeds to waste.

CHANA FAERSTEIN

The Exile

Nights in the desert, he always dreamed of voyage
and moving water, tugged by mindless tides
beyond the fixed horizon of his world;
he longed for something softer than this rock,
subtler than desert sun, cooler than sand.
Always he woke thirsting for far seas—
weary of flint rest on rocky ground,
of staring into heat-pale distances—
and holding in his hand a little dust.

—Making the voyage at last, he sinks in sleep
uneasy as water. Rock troubles his dreams,
and sun, and a desert thirst for something solid.
He cannot now remember why he sailed
or what it was he sought. Awake, he stares
at total sea. Some trick of light, or mind,
changes the long sea swell to shifting sand—
He reaches for his longing like a spar
and weeps as salt spray stings his empty hand.

MARGARET BENAYA

de Gaulle Nods Once

For greeting, de Gaulle nods once,
Then turns away unsmiling.
I too can stand aloof from the world
Like a celibate proconsul: pride,
A forest of ice, insulates me
From the encroaching gregarious city of man.
I pose with the solitary fervor
Of a pine tree shivering in an obscure backwood.
But sometimes, this damned need for warmth
Of recognition, the irrational itch
For the hot eye of the universe on my skin
And the touch of human affection on my brow
Shakes my bones like a bizarre fever.
How burn away the blood that sings
My veins to roses cursing the spiked sun?—
Agh, I break out again, green in this rash of leaves!

EUGENE BROOKS

THE MEMORY OF EDEN

They Say on Leaving Eden

they say on leaving eden eve dropped tears,
from which lilies sprang. if so, i think
these are their descendants that grow here,
with foxglove, foamflower, teasel, gentian, sloe,
lavender, and aspic, fairyfingers,
that pretty pink thats known as babys breath,
white bedstraw thats a madder, smokebush, samphire,
gaywings, loosestrife, sedum, mint, and bee balm.
its a place thats loved by chanterelles,
corkwoods, creamcups, corms of crocuses,
and by birds like avocets and stilts,
brants, turbits, and the prettiest of creatures.
no wonder, for so beautiful a setting
calls beauty into it. the gods make gods.
beauty loves to flower where its loved,
just as good thrives where its earners are,
and always pays their wages.

MARK DUNSTER

Wild Carrot

Unnoticed by the hurrying folk who pass,
The starry wild carrot blows in sun and shower
Amid the russet tangles of the grass;
Yet Heaven's garden boasts no lovelier flower.

JOHN RICHARD MORELAND

Gardening

Until the future blossoms on your limbs
And the sap blooms that pushes through your veins,
Taking its time among your growing pains,
You order in their vase chrysanthemums
Or whatever bud offers you its stem
This bursting season. Taken from the rain
The petals spread, flashing their color, wane,
Then drop upon the polished floor, like crumbs.

Before your breaking forth, I see you touch
The fallen petals, wondering if you hear
Your sighs, like shears, clipping the heart of me,
Wondering if, grown up, you'll know how much
One's blood can tremble when a child who's dear
Goes to her knees beside the flowering tree.

DABNEY STUART

Edict

From furrows of the spring,
The nut and bud are shaped,
The golden beak and wing,
The hemlock bough is draped

With bright, with living green,
The maple leaf is veined,
The violet is seen,
Its narrow petals stained.

The fountain of the snow
Melts in delicious air,
Soft light begins to blow
Down valleys that were bare.

What metamorphosis
Stirs sap and fluid fire,
To wake the clematis
And stir the branch and briar.

April remains no myth
But waking with the sun
Paints with the brush of faith
Dust and oblivion.

HAROLD VINAL

A Sunday

A child in the Sabbath peace, there—
Down by the full-bosomed river;
Sun on the tide-way, flutter of wind,
Water-cluck, Ever. . . for ever. . .

Time itself seemed to cease there—
The domed, hushed city behind me;
Home how distant! The morrow would
    come—
But here, no trouble could find me.

A respite, a solacing, deep as the sea,
Was mine. Will it come again? . . .
    Never? . . .
Shut in the Past is that Sabbath peace,
    there—
Down by the full-bosomed river.

WALTER DE LA MARE

The Fate of Elms

If they are doomed and all that can be
    done
Should fail—if they must die and dis-
    appear
And we must see them dying one by
    one,
Summer and Fall and Winter, year by
    year,
Until there comes a Summer so bereft
That over river, meadow, pasture height
No last and solitary elm is left
Lifting its leafy wings as if for flight—

Let us not make our grief for them too
    great
And say we wished that we had gone
    before,
Making the fate of elms too much our
    fate,
Seeing the always less and not the more.
Though elms may die, not everything
    must die:
Not their green memory against our sky.

ROBERT FRANCIS

Rain Song

My sad bad rain that falls
In lisp and dibble dabble
On the porch and under stairs
And puddles in the driveway brimmed
And dolloped by the slow loitering
Of the not-quite clapping hands
So slight they are on primrose
Leaves and the periwinkle
And keeps such babble going through the day.
Cats in beds sleep long
And I, I'd do the same
Or sing
If all the birds weren't gone.
It's silk under the elm leaves
It's slip into the streams
That clasp the globe around,
It's in the stealth to steal
Another tongue than bell
That does not strike but holds
All in its spell
So fresh and so small.

JEAN GARRIGUE

Siesta

The hammock swings responsive as a sail
while I abandon to its coasting all
but what I need to keep my thoughts aloof
of sunlight ricocheted from shingled roofs.

Dandled to the tempo of a pendulum
from sun to shadow, from shadow to sun,
I learn to sway no other way but slow
and hold a thought like breath, and let it go.

SAMUEL HAZO

Little Dreams

The little dreams
Of springtime
That bud in sunny air
With no roots
To nourish them,
Since no stems
Are there—
Quite detached, naive,
So young,
On air alone
Slum dreams are hung.

LANGSTON HUGHES

One A.M.

The storm came home too blind to stand,
He thwacked down oaks like chairs,
Shattered a lake and in the dark
Head over heels downstairs
Rolled, and up grumbling, on his knees,
Made nine white tries to scratch
Against walls that kept billowing
The strict head of his match.

X. J. KENNEDY

Second Blossoming

Now that the hunger born of Spring
Burned in her blood no longer,
Now that fruit
Drew its sweet milk no more from hidden root
Nor bent the heavy bough, no urgent thing
Stirred in her flesh: so must the heart grow wise,
Serene, with Summer's ending, as the skies.

But when from some high portal
Marching, the great winds blew their flaming trumpets
Till each calm hill
Rose from a burning valley to fulfill
Its dream of second blossoming, the mortal
Cry of her own dream broke against the earth
With the sharp agony of second birth.

Compassionate, she knew
In this too perfect and suspended hour
(For second dreams are brief)
Tenderness for the green, unfallen leaf.
Trembling, she touched the aster's starry blue;
And plucked the last red dahlia, petal-tossed,
From the dark fingers of the reaching frost.

RUTH LECHLITNER

Flower Arrangement

These flowers in their symmetry
Beat back the cosmic anarchy.
No commotion do they feel
From drift of sun or earth's wild reel.

Balanced here are hue and stain,
Light and shadow, curve and plane;
Nothing here is left to chance,
And change is here held in a trance.

But look! Come close! All is not tight.
Marauder ant and petal blight
Drop speckles of betraying dust.
See on this leaf the touch of rust!

SAMUEL YELLEN

Toward Harvest

Making our late world whole, we grow to see
Apples like fat October in a tree

Still green and perfect on its darkening bole
As the round fruit it bears: for round is whole.

The scent of apples waxes with the moon
And longer nights; and often, now, at noon

The simple sunlight slants like falling frost
Across the orchard. Nothing yet is lost;

Though apples bend the branches to the ground,
They ripen still. The world grows truly round.

Only when one warm Northern Spy lets go
Are we aware of change to come, like snow.

SAMUEL FRENCH MORSE

Rain

The parts of trees,
leaves, twigs and moving boughs,
reveal the wind.

But rain can be most surely gauged
on the surface of still water.
The punctured holes
make clear the congregation of the drops,
and each circumference the size
and force is manifest
in brief beads popping
above the spreading circles
linking the water
in a coat of living mail.

ROSS PARMENTER

The Feel of Fineness

Heavy carnations and the small ancestral pinks
Lace jagged odor, shape, and color through the air
And with an aromatic sharpness bear
A spiced renewal to the one who drinks
Their pungent brightness through the senses, taught
To dream thereby of eastern splendor or the dawn
Waking small flowers by a liquid stretch of lawn
Or little blooms by Lowland painters wrought
To place precision in a pincer hand.
In every case, there is a feel of line
In clean conjunction with a colored scent,
A thin-edged beauty, layered over land,
Swift through a lurking mistiness and fine
As is your own directness to its missions bent.

JOHN HAZARD WILDMAN

A Blade of Grass

Between the gutter and sidewalk
   A blade of grass up stood—
It was greener than the color
   And lonelier than the blood.
But the odds piled up against it
   Was a fact it could not own,
There was certainty in its angle
   As it took that wave of stone,
And cut right through the armor,
   Vegetation's miracle sword,

As the first step of the era
   It surely was aiming toward.
It honed against the wind
   An edge of utter blade,
And in the earth's large hand
   It whispered unafraid—
Not so's ears could hear it—
   Though your eyes could never doubt
It was a piercing of perfection
   Which had stretched the long street out.

OSCAR WILLIAMS

Dewdrop

Blue in a lupin-leaf
after-dawn diamond
unliquidly
shone

A simple brilliant
eating the face of
the morning
sun

A crystal of night as
hard as star-glint
fixed as owl-eye

Closing upon some inner
darkness tinily
it mirrored
me.

TED WALKER

Flower of "The Living Desert"

It is too sudden
For our sluggard sight
This unfolding flower:
The time compressed,
The blossom magnified,
By cunning lens.

Too swift the petals
Come unshuttered;
The huddled stamens quivering
Pale creatures of the dark
Exposed to a fierce light.

Watching a crimson bud
Flare to a fiery disk,
Its beauty bursting like a cry—
We came too close to hidden marvel
Uncovered by a cold and convex eye.

MARY WINTER

The Manzanita

Under the forest, where the air is dark
And all but motionless throughout the
    day,
Rooted in leaf-mold and in rotting bark,
This old arbutus gathers strength to
    stay.

Tall as a man, and taller, but more old,
This is no shrub of some few years, but
    hard
Its smooth unbending trunk, oh, hard
    and cold!
Of earth and age, the stony proof and
    guard!

The skin is rose: yet infinitely thin,
It is a color only. What one tells
Of ancient wood or softly glinting skin
Is less than are the tiny waxen bells.

This life is not our life; nor for our wit
The sweetness of these shades; these are
    alone.
There is no wisdom here: seek not for it!
This is the shadow of the vast madrone.

                                YVOR WINTERS

The Peace of Wild Things

When despair for the world grows in me
and I wake in the night at the least sound
in fear of what my life and my children's lives may be,
I go and lie down where the wood drake
rests in his beauty on the water, and the great heron feeds.
I come into the peace of wild things
who do not tax their lives with forethought
of grief. I come into the presence of still water.
And I feel above me the day-blind stars
waiting with their light. For a time
I rest in the grace of the world and am free.

WENDELL BERRY

Rain

Water stumbles after its own level
Going where it goes going down:
Whether to veins, seams in limestone,
To sea and cloud, it moves in travail.

Undersides of leaves blacken, paving flares,
Dark lightens, lights darken with this rain:
Where the street pips or waves to cars
Toy boats race the gutter down to the storm drain.

It's half life falling, still almost pure,
Purer still as light breaks after laying on hands,
Splatters, moves in a wave to the next star,
Pure theory almost, except in the hands of friends.

LOUIS COXE

"MORTALITY WEIGHS HEAVILY ON ME . . ."

Conversation with a Friend

My friend, the talks I have with you
are that bright orchard snarl of limbs
I stole through as a thieving boy
for the crab-apple's crimply taste,
knob-pithy pinkness yielding strict
and bitter beauty of stolen feast.

Thus from the harsh and canny yield
of your life's webbing stamped by sun
I filch those stingy mercies full
which grant a quick and acid power
the juices of my heart can turn
through all the branches of my year.

Relaxed, conversing, we make our air
an orchard texture of woven word,
the august from sullen, wit from dour,
gladness from both. Yet all the while
I sense a watcher, the boyhood curse,
the neighbor-owner; and this one smiles

as lemon-taut, as pronged with stare
as she in window, frail and fierce,
who watched, fingering the glass with mild
and childish hands. And this is decay—
mortality, who owns and peers.

GEORGE ABBE

Small Elegy

Say that she was young, awkward and bold—
Light matured her virtues some few summers
Then set her down; oh the promise
Of her dawn, the wide expectant eye.

Or write of her voice, uncertain as a reed
But supple with high faith; death stopped
It. Now the riderless seasons
Race and change, shrouded in speed.

MORRIS WEISENTHAL

The Dust of Love

Where are they now, the lovely dust
In Tristram's eyes and Abelard's?
The centuries will do for guards.
Bracelet and sword are weak with rust.

Where are the singers, shaping words
To will old yearning ever fresh?
They went the way of honored flesh.
Above them sing the fellow birds.

Deep in the grave the husband lies,
His jealousy consumed in sleep.
The watchful father slumbers deep
Beyond the closed and peaceful eyes.

Somewhere in some eternal now
The lovers smile a fleeting greeting
And courteously confirm the meeting,
A curtsy measured to a bow.

CHAD WALSH

Polemic

Now you have made a perfect new
World inside your head,
My friend, look your last at that view.
The world you never made is true.

All you shun can yet undo
That world you love instead
Of Man. Good friend, you misconstrue
The world you never made for rue.

You cannot lie alone. Unto
The last, narrow bed,
Good Man, Man is Man's just due.
The world you never made is you.

ANTHONY OSTROFF

Fiftieth Birthday

Only less sure of all I never knew.
Always more awed by what is never new.
Computer, spare the mustang's randomness.

There was an oracle. On Samothrace?
There have been tablets. Here? Some greener place?
I (leaf) paint leaves that (falling) try to dance.

Have seen the big death, felt the little death:
The icy and the April breathlessness.
And understand them less and less and less.

Have met the loam-fed and the plastic wreath:
Statesman and hack. Two frightening frightened boys.
Both more endearing than the consequence.

Have heard your rebels and have heard your guild:
And still can't tell the standard from the stance
When both are so rehearsed a cheering noise.

Have squandered silver and have hoarded pence.
Have watched the ant-hill build, burn up, rebuild
(The running is and isn't meaningless)

At Ilium. Or will it be South Bend?
I'll grudge the run a meaning in the end
When wounds that might wound back or else "transcend"

Have risked—instead—to be. Not even bless.

PETER VIERECK

What the Wind Said

White bone clinging to white bone
In their marriage bed,
Haven and shield against menacing weather,
Shivered to hear what the wind said:
"Soon, soon, you must lie alone,
Torn like leaves from an autumn bough,
But till nightfall you may twine together
As you do now."

White bone resting on white bone
In their common grave,
Safe and sealed against menacing weather,
Were deaf to the comfort the wind gave:
"Nevermore shall you lie alone,
But close as leaves on a summer bough
Till the world's end you may twine together
As you do now."

JOHN PRESS

The Broken Kaleidoscope

Nothing stays so long that it
May not in an instant flit.
Quench the candle, gone are all
The wavering shadows on the wall.
Watch now, Sweet, your image here
In this water, calm and fair;
Speedwell eye and amber hair—
See, I fling a pebble in,
What distortions now begin;
Refluent ripples sweep and sway,
Chasing all your charms away,
Now, imagine a strange glass
Which at look gave back, alas,
Nothing but a crystal wall,
And else, no hint of you at all:
No rose on cheek, no red on lip,
No trace of beauty's workmanship.
That, my dear, for me and you,
Precisely is what life might do—
Might, I say. Oh, then how sweet
Is it by this stream to sit,
And in its molten mirror see
All that is now reality:
The interlacing boughs, the sun's
Tiny host of flickering moons,
That rainbow kingfisher, and these
Demure, minute anemones,
Cherubim, in heaven's blue,
Leaning their wizard faces, too—
Lost in delight at seeing you.

WALTER DE LA MARE

Ritual

(Oscawana Lake, N. Y.)

The descending swans
spread the umbrella of their wings
over copse and lake,
on the fringes of which I sit, initiate.
It is a morning and evening ritual.
Time too has its ritual:
in the slow descent of the hours,
in the folding of imperceptible wings,
under the shadow of which I wait.

GUSTAV DAVIDSON

Rings in a Roundness

Here rounds our ring, the wheel of earth's horizon.
Along these raying spokes our light is laid.
Here from this hub we may set out with eyes on
All distance down the paths all lives have made,
And come at length to what seemed once earth's ending,
Then look again, and find, as found before,
The same near earth, the same far sky's blue bending,
No less than seen, of all we sensed no more.

Life is like this, going on, going on forever,
But beginning and ending always in us who bend
Into rings within a roundness, who are never
Nearer our origin than our own end.

CARLETON DREWRY

R. G. E.

A new desire to understand
Took hold on me and drove my hand
To prove my own identity
By digging letters on a tree.

"The maple tree will bear my scar
When I have grown and traveled far."
I said it blithely as a boy.
I carved the wood with eager joy,
Gouging my three initials deep
And deeper still, so they would keep.
It was an impulse when alone
To clarify the vague, half-known
Surmise I had that I was part
Of trees and knew them in my heart.
It was believing that the tree
Would be forever nearer me
That made me cut away the bark
And trench the maple with my mark.

Brutal the clod who feels no sting
In injuring a perfect thing.
The maple felt a primal shame
To bear the imprint of my name.
It only wanted sustenance.
It felt no need of permanence,
Because it knew the earth and stood
All day in quiet brotherhood.
But I was racked and torn. Hot pain
Shot through and tingled in my brain
And would not cease, because I knew
Truth that hurt me through and through.
Never can our human will
Be calm and tree-like, free and still.

RICHARD EBERHART

Old Women Remember

They only seem to forget:
nothing is forgotten really.
Love comes back, the rack of birth returns,
and withered cheeks are wet
with tears that runnel newly.
On folded hands the scalding water burns.
They remember the flesh,
its myriad hungers waking,
and heaviness, for love is a weight to bear.
A child is cradled afresh,
and love, at the child's making.
Women are crushed by weight no longer there.

ROSALIE BOYLE

In the Hospital

I have been long away
from the electric hills
locked in my own anatomy.
The brain's a stuffy attic.
Here I've foraged
a long while out of the sun,
chewing the old clothes
of scholarship, a dry moth.
Now I fly through the window.
This is the way moths die:
drowned by the sun
or snapped up by a humming bird.
So be it.

DILYS LAING

Nerves

The wind is playing round the curtains,
The bowl of flowers throws shadows on the sill.
There is nothing to do now, nothing at all
But to lie still.

The mind has never been like this room, clear,
Containing only what I really need.
It has been full of antique objects, rubbish,
And dust indeed.

The objects seemed to swell, their shadows spread
More darkness than I knew how I could handle.
There was no sudden shock, simply a slow
Feeling that strength would dwindle,

That I would one day find myself like this—
Lying in bed, watching the curtains blow,
Seeing the petals fall, petal by petal,
Longing for something to grow.

ELIZABETH JENNINGS

My Face Looks Out

My face looks out to take the world as it
Has always been: low-keyed, intelligible
to the unreasoned eye, acceptable,
except as now it comes to me that it
is almost fifty years since I am able
so casually to look with eyes that take
the whole world in or any part I'd make
into something of my own a while.

Nothing I do or have done earns this right.
It just is. Eyes by being eyes have sight;
if nothing hinders, light pours through endlessly.
It is for me to make of what eyes see
a curbstone, passing dog, gigantic tree.
Who says, "Are all I see lost parts of me?"

EDWIN HONIG

Farm Couple, After Norman Rockwell

They walk against a hueless sky
With heads tipped up on tautened strings.
And now the snow begins to fly,
Now snow preens out its earthwide wings
And flurries in a stir so sweet
They pause in awe on homeward feet
As if the Angel Death were white.
Does either guess the other feels
A dark behind the day that night
Itself but fitfully conceals?

BARRY SPACKS

The Return

Go back from pistons to the plod of hooves;
Go back from hooves to inching of the worm;
Return from footed motion to the rose,
To where the rose unfolds from bud to bloom:
Slower than roses is the going in the earth.

The reaches of the sun into bleached acres,
Its fingers grinding the scalp under the grass,
The phantom tap of moon from star to star
Are legends of a farther India
No ocean travels on its currents home.

Here only the darkness shedding its own light;
Here only the fold of hands upon themselves,
The soundlessness whence ears are to be born
To hear the giant ants from arch to arch
Advance like whirlwind with their load of mountains.

What sentences are spoken by the rain:
Let fall, like slowly myth, from mouth to mouth?
What whisper of the mist, the ghost of rain?
What frosty word? What merely mumbling stone
Withholds its jealousies from common ground?

Beside the immigrant oaks that till the rock,
The baffled way of willow after water,
What memories escaping from the nerve
Are spent into that larger vagary
Whose memory is more than birth and death?

In a new season, where the roots commune
Whose thoughts lie near the now unthinking head,
What summons from the air, like foreign blood,
Will rally the reactionary dead
Up out of their loamed forgetfulness?

LLOYD FRANKENBERG

The Dead Branch

A sun-bleached skeleton
The dead branch had become,
Wind-tossed like an old bone
To lie in the deep ditch
As songless as a stone
Until I took it home.

I gave it to the fire,
And saw it spring and twitch
With passionate desire,
And phoenix-like, a flare
Lit up the darkening air,
As at the hour of death
Some long-imprisoned thing
Will conjure back its breath,
And suddenly sing
Of how when green and young
Its sensuous beauty through the sweet air swung.

DOUGLAS GIBSON

Old Woman Sitting in the Sun

No-life drags on in the shuttered heart;
The mind gropes back through memory's loss
To memories of Never-was,
Where voices, shapes, old music dart
Like shimmering fish in a caverned sea
With never a forward wave.
Only the swell of a darkling past
That surges endlessly.

Gray monolith of time,
Passive, petrified, still, in your deep unknowing!
The children's cries in their lusty play
Pass you by like a white wind blowing,
Blowing the brooding clouds apart;
But no light falls on the hooded brain,
On the shuttered heart.

MARY L. INMAN

The Lace Maker

Needle, needle open up
The convolvulus of your eye,
I must come upon it quick
Or my thread will die.

Night is settling down outside,
My sallow candle seems to thin,
But I must weave this laddered thread
To nest each rare space in.

It is dark. Darkness plaits a scarf
Over my eyes. Can finger sprout
Eyes at the tip to guide its work?
. . . . Each evening, I go out

To Sainte Gudule—if I can see
Needlepoint of aspiring stone,
The window's rose embroidery
Trained like a trumpet upon Heaven,

Then I may live; but if my sight
Narrows toward death, a black-a-vised
Gargoyle will jut out, grinning there,
Exulting in that swirling mist.

BARBARA HOWES

It's Somebody's Birthday

This birthday man
Rises from my hot bed
Into his mirror.
When I groan
Out of his crumpled head
He prods my dewlap with a jeering finger.
Behind his eyes
Lie the slim silver boys
Called by my name.
No blind surprise
Nor moving without noise
Shall ever startle them inside that frame.
To my round skin
He will remain flat true
Warning for warning.
I pull my stomach in,
March a hard step or two,
Shut loud the bathroom door, murder his morning.

LESLIE NORRIS

Olduvai

Seeing in illustrated magazines
Artists' conceptions of primordial man
(Older than Adam by a day of ages,
Yet less equivocal than apes with tools),
We brood upon the bearded face that means
Our minds and aristocracies began
In human terms so constant all our stages
Were scarcely more than inefficient schools;
And, if we could, we would deny the light
Linking those murky eyes and our clear own
With wonder at the sun and the hawk's flight;
But pity and nostalgia bend our sight
Till we perceive as with the very bone,
As autumn comes and we grow cold at night.

LEROY SMITH, JR.

After Seeing "Lear"

The Home for Senior Citizens, the heath
On which they wander, mad and maddening,
The dreadful old:
She wants to queen it still in her two rooms,
Dishevelled, fumbling for authority
Over the gas stove that she cannot light;
And he wants to be heard.

"Reason not the need."

Poor Goneril, poor Regan!
Who can heed
Imperious decay, beseeching, bold?
Better lock fast the gate, deafen the ear
To that impossible cry;
Close tight the shutters on the storm of age,
That feeble fury beating at our peace.

MARIE SYRKIN

AS THROUGH
A GLASS DARKLY

The Rider

In the morning,
The mist still formed,
A chill in the air,
The long stands empty,
We leaned at the railing
With our steaming cup of hands
That held the coffee's heat

When there came through the distance
Upon a horse slowly pacing,
With slow rocking gait,
A rider strange seeming,
Bent over on the seat,
Who had let drop the reins—
With face asleep or veiled—

Whom we would have called across the space—

Except for the crop
Which stuck stiffly up
And impaled the slumped body
Nodding as it came
Metronomically toward us
As it would not stop but overwhelm us
On its steed across the smoldering sod

WILLIAM BURFORD

The Bear

Voices ring out. Branches whip the air
With the heavy swish of bow strings
And huge shadows are cast against the stars.
Waking, something rolls underfoot and you spin

Far from the bottom of sleep, tractionless,
Your feet in the trees, your head in the needles.
The dark smudge of a bear's face mingles
With boulders and flows into the darkness

As if it recedes into the darkness
Of its own fat. Then the trees stand still;
Shadows run down like tops and spill
Away. The severed tries to reassemble.

The ground is strewn with a flock of echoes
And you listen to the bear, deep
In shadow and dissolved among stones
Where he walks, now, on another's sleep.

JOHN RANDELL CARPENTER

Lost Days

Then, when an hour was twenty hours, he lay
Drowned in deep grass. He watched the carrier ant,
With mandibles as trolley, push in front
Wax yellow specks across the parched cracked clay.

A tall sun made the stems down there transparent.
Shifting, he saw the speedwell's sudden eye
Start up close to his own, a chink of sky
Cut through the deep tarpaulin of a tent.

He pressed his mouth against the rooted ground.
Held in his arms, he felt the earth spin round.

STEPHEN SPENDER

Retreat

Now as we fall back from below the ridge,
Abandoning our hotly held positions,
We can lay aside the anguish of our fear
And assume the duller burden of ourselves.
For though our dead are carefully interred,
Their honor well established, and although
The military manuals positively state
That such assaults as ours can never win,
And though we knew the odds against success
Were infinite, still we must explain—
Explain the failure of the bayonet,
The fury of the enfilading fire,
Explain the lack of mortars and air cover.
We must explain, and once again explain,
That no defect of ours, no lack of courage,
No failure of the nerve or of the will
Repulsed our thrusts. We must refight this field
Forever on the ridges of our minds
And lose it always as we lost it here.

J. K. CLARK

Mount Parnassus

Never have I been in the south
So far from self and yet I must
Learn, straight from the horse's mouth
To kick up my own dust.
Here is the source. Here was our must.
I see no flowers to grass us,
Only the scale of Mount Parnassus:
Simplicity of snow
Above, the pillared drouth,
The worn-out, below.
I stray from American, German, tourists,
Greek guide, feel in my two wrists
Answer for which I have come,
The Oracle, not yet dumb.

AUSTIN CLARKE

Cross Talk

"Himself on the Wood there," says one,
"is surely the Son of His Mother,
a Man done undoing what's done."
"He could be Himself," says another.

Said she, "He's Himself is my own,
Himself only, born to be given,
bled whitest, white Bread of my bone,
red liveliest Wine for all living."

CYRIL CUSACK

Picasso's "Portrait de Femme"

Perhaps on such a day as this—but
In France in 1936, before,
That is, the War and other events
Now too infinite to list (though
Out-of-doors the oak whispers not
And the birds exist much as
They did and will) came and went
Like that and like this, all things
That time bore and then dismissed
—Before the War perhaps, on such
A day, as this, Dora Maar (let us
Say, "Dora Maar," for who would be
Anonymous? and her name was all
She really wore) sat in a chair
In 19 and 36 with a wish fierce
And commonplace to be mysterious,
To survive and to thrive, to be a success
And be good, and be covered
With paint like a kiss,
Eternally, in nineteen hundred thirty-six.

IRVING FELDMAN

I, a Justified Sinner

Crossed bridges before I got to them.
Always burned them after me.
Invariably lay in a bed of my own making,
Single or double, it made do.
Slept the sleep of the blessed.
Rose on the right side mostly,
Otherwise, the other.
Followed the strait and narrow
As it suited me.
Chose my own companions,
Cherished them as they deserved.
Served others as I myself was served.
Honey or gall,
I took my fare unfailingly with salt
Knew myself as well as anyone.
Lord who made such marvels,
   Lord who fashioned me,
Thank you for your mercies;
   Now give your grace to me.
   The day when I shall not arise,
Let me rise up to Thee.
   On Thy side Lord, the right side,
Trust me to trust in Thee!

ARNOLD PRICE

Ceremony

The hour suggested offerings,
a grateful gesture, being day of goldleaf light,
thin overleaf of sun, bright without heat.

In a garden leaning toward its sleep,
I cut chrysanthemums; red, yellow, white.

From summer's hoard I chose five stones
brought from the sea, smooth ovals and rounds.

Celebrant of a season gone,
I made slow ritual of forms;
the golden bowl, oblation of water,
brilliant flowers held upright by dark stones.

It was done—but for a music, seeming magic,
unexpected water-whistle, soprano, bubbling bass.
Five thirsty sea-wrenched stones drank to their fill,
gulped and grew black, grew heavy as summer,
sang, and were still.

                                    JOANNE DE LONGCHAMPS

Boys Will Be Princes

Once upon a time, was a place
we knew, rotting its columns, where
lay a beauty, dreamed her lovely face,
ogre-spelling and tranced in sleeping there.

Became her Charmings, searched its corridor
to find her hidden chamber and break
its ugly haunt, and walked the dusty floor
leaving witches dead as curtains in our wake.

Once upon a was, beat its mirrors in
to thinner, smaller ghosts, where
fell they there, a dark and silver din
to threaten any castle's awesome air.

Courage, honor, chivalry at stake
and all her captured loveliness.
Found a stairway, climbed it for the sake
of slaying all the darkness we could guess

was guarding her in goblin, dragon guise,
deceptive fairy shape, or spin
of web from some despotic Merlin's eyes.
Her golden hair, her breath, her lips to win.

Upon a time, kicked an enchanted door
and was a woman, livid there,
some ragged hag, aghast, clutching at her dress,
screaming curses, and pulling at her hair.

WILLIAM HEYEN

Rapunzel Song

Upon the slow descending air
the trees let down their darkened hair;
the leaves are falling, so the night
turning away from what's more bright
may come as a lover to the shade,
wearing the wind.

So once the maid
Rapunzel of the legends found
she'd lifted a lover from the ground
who by her hair, that yellow flame,
ascended.

Who now knows his name?
And was he dark or was he fair?
Only, upon the lovely stair
he met Rapunzel.

Of the night
what more is known, than: on the slight
and windy tresses of the trees
a dark gallant was seen to seize,
amorously began to climb
and mounted swiftly into time.

GERARD PREVIN MEYER

Homecoming

Having both daughters at home does not give me
a very merry Christmas. Tall in the hall
they brush past mythic photos of their small
selves in camping days. Though they do love me
(in some new way now), it would ill behoove me
to fold them in my arms: satirical
silences from their scholarly eyes would fall.
Even their songbursts, their fits of laughter, grieve me.

Outside my window through the wide sky swarm
clouds that seem to know more than they are saying.
No comfort this night, when hailstorms lash, to hear
both daughters breathing safely: what of the storm
next week? what of the storm next month? next year?
how will they be dressed? where will they be staying?

AARON KRAMER

The Unbroken Code

Agent of obscure
powers, countries whose names, whose
locations even, he

cannot now recall.
As he cannot distinguish,
some days, his real

from his coded name.
Or say why he carries that
map of broken veins

inside his ankle,
who no longer knows he cares,
or cares if he knows

where its roads may lead.
His contact missed, dead perhaps,
he waits for someone

to speak the word he
will remember the ring of,
key to his reason

for being there on
the cheap brass bed by the phone,
in the soaking dark

of Playa del Sol.

ROBERT DANA

To Somewhere

This is the road to Somewhere—
All feet and all hooves
That take it, and all wheels,
Set out for something rare:
The water's source, beauty's riches,
Or one truth in God's many names.
On the way, flies for companions,
The skin, like a separate beast, twitches,
And men brush their streaming eyes,
But see no better through the dust
That cartwheels turn up in a delirious
Riverbed of hot days.
Sometimes, its windows shut tight,
A royal car swerves by, destined
For the beggar's black ditch ahead.
The travellers pass it at midnight,
Emptied of purpose, and they don't care;
They've forgotten all but going, forgotten
The goods that set them forth; in truth,
Forgotten how to stop, but will somewhere.

LEONARD E. NATHAN

Coexistence

Grant the gray cat
Find a warm sunning
Far from the bird,
Young, without cunning,
That fell.

May the mute fish
Dart past the baited
Rod—and the angler
Homeward go sated
As well.

Foolish the wish,
Human in error,
While the soft worm
Writhing in terror,
Hangs there unheard.

MARIE SYRKIN

Tanist

Remember the spider
Weaving a snare
—And that you did it
Everywhere:

Remember the cat
Tormenting a bird
—And that you did it
In deed and word:

Remember the fool
Frustrating the good
—And that you did it
Whenever you could:

Remember the devil
And treachery
—And that you did it
When you were he:

Remember all ill,
That man can know
—And that you did it
When you were so:

And then remember
Not to forget
—That you did it,
And do it yet.

JAMES STEPHENS

Look, See the Cat

A bird's wing lies under your swing.
The cat cleans her face in a sunny place.
The mother bird screams. This is the first
lesson, but not the worst,
though a child turns cold in the sunny place
where the cat cleans her face.

Now you scream with the bird. The sleek, furred
cat could never be you. Lesson two
is the long look you turn to the dark inside
places where cats hide.
Look, see the cat. This is lesson two:
the cat could be you.

The Ruthless Moon

The ruthless moon is halfway through its arc
And in the draw the secret prowlers creep
As ruthless as the moon. In the grassy dark
A fox falls on a rabbit that huddles asleep.
There is no cry; the grass is broken and bent
And flagged with fur, but not bowed down with ruth
For the rabbit slain, it is as indifferent
To that death as the moon that glints from the fox's tooth.
But the man stands fixed and gazing into the draw
Where the narrow fox feasts on the downy dead;
He sees the shadowy lion leap, the law
Made flesh; and the fox lie forfeit where the rabbit bled;
And in a terror of ruth his shocked heart beats
Alike for the terrible flesh he is and eats.

Job

And God said, How do you know?
And I went out into the fields
At morning, and it was true.

Nothing denied it, neither the bowed man
On his knees, nor the animals,
Nor the birds, notched on the sky's

Surface. His heart was broken
Far back; and the beasts yawned
Their boredom. Under the song

Of the larks, I heard the wheels turn
Rustily. But the scene held.
The cold landscape returned my stare.

There was no answer: Accept. Accept.
And under the green capitals—
The molecules and the blood's virus.

R. S. THOMAS

The Aquarium Dream

Teeters on the top of the stairs,
Spirals down through fog that clears
Around the windows that reveal
Gaping goldfish, sinuous eels,
Ventral flounders, profile sharks,
Then, unwary, bumps on the dark
Floor of sliding sand that pulls

The dreamer toward a final wall
Where glass holds in a flood of green
And murky water. First it seems
The tank is empty; then a hulk
Surges forward through the muck
Of its own churning. Head on crowds
The giant turtle. Her widening mouth
Smacks, rattles the glass. Her eyes
Blaze hate and hunger, recognize
That aspirant who crawled ashore
To cover dry ground, displace air,
And furtively returns to stare.

FLORENCE TREFETHEN

Queer Poem

I knew a man without a heart:
Boys tore it out, they said,
And gave it to a hungry wolf
Who picked it up and fled.

And fled the boys, their masters too,
All distant fled the brute,
And after it, in quaint pursuit,
The heartless man reeled on.

I met this man the other day
Walking in grotesque pride.
His heart restored, his mien gay,
The meek wolf by his side.

MALCOLM LOWRY

They See Dark Skies

They see dark skies of unshed snow behind
The snow-sleeved trees like dancers touching hands.
The northern frontier. Vast unfriendly lands
Far from the groves of red and golden rind
Where, in alfresco schools the cogent mind
Hatched a philosophy that brought these bands
Of civilizing privates—fate none understands.
To think there is another, strange, mankind!

So nearly indistinguishable from
Barbarians, the inhabitants, that for long
Their masters goggle with inquietude
At women with their hair like pelts, snow-strewed,
Until they are, insidiously as song,
Possessed and haunted by the idiom.

ROY FULLER

"HAVE PITY
ON US, POWER . . ."

Prayer

Have pity on us, Power just and severe,
　　Have pity on our greed, our hate, our lust,
And on our endless anxieties, our ugly fear.
　　Great Wisdom, grant wisdom to this timid dust.

Have patience with us, who have betrayed one another
　　And parted the single and seamless robe of man,
And divided his garments among us, who is our brother.
　　Infinite Patience, have patience if You can.

Have mercy on us—because we are merciless
　　And have need of mercy, all other needs above—
And on our angry littleness,
　　Pity Inexorable, Remorseless Love.

JOHN HALL WHEELOCK

Fellow-creatures

The heart shall not be satisfied
Until all creatures hear its word;
The lion's love must be its pride,
Its joy the friendship of a bird.

It would be welcome in the lairs
Of lynxes, and lie down with them,
Would lean upon the sides of bears,
Stroke the wild peacock's diadem,

Confer with singing seals in caves,
With the tall ostrich in the sand,
And where the long liana waves
Touch the great ape's accomplished hand.

How shall the heart such rapture reach
Till the stiff tongue its manners mend,
To say to men, in human speech,
"Beloved, immortal spirit, friend"?

RUTH PITTER

From "Suite in Prison"

Lord, stabilize me. My legs
Fail in the white crevasses. My hands
To thin husks are twisted. My bones
In the high winds can stand no more.

Blood that built the heavy world
Curls in the shells it built,
Thins and congeals. Its cold heart
Would turn to the earth, its home.

Eyes, the last levelers of the world,
Have lost direction and show false,
The rare air them avails
With many ways of ice and snow.

Of glassy temples crinkling white,
Glittering all the icy air,
As cold a city and as bright
As flicks in the tight air of a child.

Lord, stabilize me. My pride
Walks with inebriate legs. My desire
Eats up the whole world. My love
In its big excess destroys me.

Lord, qualify me. To see
Pride floored like a marionette;
Desire fulfilled like a marriage;
And love of sweet use in the world.

Lord, admit me. To rejoice
Even within the abysm of suffering.
Contain me in Thine atmosphere, Lord.
And in the dancing of Thine ecstasy.

RICHARD EBERHART

The Calvaries

On Breton heaths the village craftsmen's hands
Portrayed in stone
Their peasant Calvaries,
Where Breton Christs
Are bowed beneath the weight
Of crosses weathered
By the centuries
And tears in stone are washed
By wind-borne rain,
As Pardons kneel
By wild Atlantic shores.
The craftsman's faith
Four hundred years ago
Knocked love in stone, and every blow
Remains
To match each single blow
That falls today
In villages
Five thousand miles away.

PETER WILLIAMSON

Cry for a Dead Soldier

O God of Strength, fabled Omnipotence,
Who brought from chaos all these intricate shapes
And fashioned them to beauty and to use,
Look now upon this dead—
Make recompense!
Take in your Hand this twisted caricature;
Reknit the bone, reshape the shattered limb;
Make fast again the broken ligature.
Lift up the foot's fair arch, the smooth, lean flank;
Remold the lips' firm curves.
Reweave
The delicate tendrils of the shredded nerves,
The brain's fine filaments, in true design.
Retrieve
The bright blood spilled from artery and vein.
Bring back the light gone from those staring eyes,
And blow your breath once more into the lung.
Oh, recognize
This man! and raise him up, proud, beautiful, and young.
Restore his voice and his familiar name,
And set him striding your eternal ways,
Transfigured from this flesh, and yet the same;
Unchanged from his inimitable mold,
Never to alter—never to grow old.

MARY L. INMAN

Praise to the Stutterer

Praise to the blocked word
of the stutterer, stumbling
out of the mute might
of the rock which Moses hit,
to quench the scorched wilderness.

No, not the rainbow
of the bubble, bragging it
is a gold planet
flying to replace the sun:
the pomp of charmed nothingness.

The word which falters
seeing God face to face, rocks
ages of bondage,
stammers like thunder as it
rolls to applaud the cosmos.

MENKE KATZ

Graves at Inishbofin

(*Ireland*)

St. Colman came from Lindisfarne
And here built his abbey.
He cut an altar out of stone
Eastward facing the sea,
Under whose shawl the voice of Mary
Answered his antiphon.

The wind has blown away his prayers
Leaving a wild graveyard
Where carried by the islanders
Come those who've died,
The drowned (if got) and the black-shawled
Go under these boulders.

RICHARD MURPHY

Symbolism

I do not mind symbolism;
Christ playing peek-a-boo
between a poem's postulates,

or a lady on canvas who holds
a pomegranate on her palm
(stood up by the local garbage truck).

It is the things that enter and leave
abruptly as Lear's fool—
a face pivoted against backs of heads,
bewildered in the newsreel mob,
turning singly to question the camera—

midnight on the subway I watch
an old woman fall asleep
against the handle of her new rake.
But it is mid-summer.
Whom does she have for leaves?

KAREN SWENSON

Saint Francis

II

In the flare of rose-bed
splendor he stands anew,
as if a plaster saint
could will himself to flesh
and bone and walk from their
backyard to mine. Ah no,
they came again last night,
devilish boys with Halloween
still up their sleeves.

Yet what they did was more
like love than any prank
they sprang and howled
before; and this, what's more,
was done in silence softer
than the night they hid behind.

Today no wind blows and the
spring sun is brilliant over
land and sea, an assurance
perhaps, that what was done
the saint condoned with joy.

I've a mind to leave him
there, so elegantly oblivious
among the clouds of rose
and green, deeply involved
with the soft-sent coo

of a dove upon his wrist,
while the sun drinks holy
water from round his feet
like a blinding flock
of thirsty birds.

ROGER PFINGSTON

Song of the Withy Greatcoat

By dusk on shore he's waiting,
under an osier's cover,
wrapped in a withy greatcoat
on the one lone edge of river.

Turns inland, the late comer,
takes one more breastful of clover.
In an hour he's bound homeward
from the single side of river.

Turns back to kneel in aster.
In mauve twilight the traveler,
hooded in willow, one last time
rears back from the half-bound river.

Draws close his woven greatcoat.
Calls out though the withes shiver:
Come cross me, steady boatman,
over the one-strand river!

NORMA FARBER

By One, Unsure

My feet toe in, as Indians' do,
A natural gait,
And as I track across the snow,
Pursuing fate,
My thoughts turn inward, shutting out
The world's distractions roundabout.

I pause a step and gaze behind
To note a pattern well defined,
Stampings from a special mint
As personal as fingerprint.

The course between, a winding path
Of strait and unassuming breadth,
By one, unsure of destinies,
Who swerves within parentheses.

MELVILLE CANE

The Supplanting

Where the road came, no longer bearing men,
but briars, honeysuckle, buckbush and wild grape,
the house fell to ruin, and only the old wife's daffodils
rose in spring among the wild vines to be domestic
and to keep the faith, and her peonies drenched the tangle
with white bloom. For a while in the years of its wilderness
a wayfaring drunk slept clinched to the floor there
in the cold nights. And then I came, and set fire
to the remnants of house and shed, and let time
hurry in the flame. I fired it so that all
would burn, and watched the blaze settle on the waste
like a shawl. I knew those old ones departed
then, and I arrived. As the fire fed, I felt rise in me
something that would not bear my name—something that
    bears us
through the flame, is lightened of us, and is glad.

WENDELL BERRY

Ego

If enemies amputate
both hands and arms,
I still walk
across a summer ground,
and, legless, I can see
the world revolve.
Blind, my mouth will sing
beyond my eyes.
Tongue torn out,
I shall hear
the season turn.
When I am deaf
to my own cries,
and the visions
in my own mind chill,
this heart will beat
like the world's own clock.
And when for want of winding
the works run down,
no man dies;
it's the world that stops.

A. KIRBY CONGDON

Thrush for Hawk

From thicket, thrush,
Quick in a flush to flight
His purl in harsh brush
Was, as his flash to light
And soar to height
Is what we wish for, might
Wing, to bushed heart's hush,
Rise, when bleak is hawk blight
Over us, night.

JOHN FANDEL

The Doll

Dollmaker, snug in your house
with your shelf piled with dolls, how can
you sleep? Yesterday in the grass
I saw, with her head full of bran
and her eyes one dead blue stare,
a doll that a child had flung
down carelessly, running off elsewhere
with a shrieking, living tongue.
But careless of that neglect,
she simpered as she lay,
still stiffly circumspect
beneath the changing day.
And if she blushed, it was not
anger or shame for that fickle child—
merely a painted spot.
She would drive no parents wild,
whose cry was a built-in cry,
and not for pleasure, not for woe.
Not from that wax thigh
would the thick blood flow.

Dollmaker, do you not fear
that on the Judgment Day,
her limbs will begin to stir
and her Cupid lips say:
"He has much to answer for,
who to satisfy his pride,
out of wax, paint and straw,
insolently has made,
though with a craftsman's art,
this body I could not live,
perfect, without a heart
to suffer and forgive."

ROBERT FRIEND

At a Child's Baptism

Hold her softly, not for long
Love lies sleeping on your arm,
Shyer than a bird in song,
Quick to fly off in alarm.

It is well that you are wise,
Knowing she for whom you care
Is not yours as prey or prize,
No more to be owned than air.

To your wisdom you add grace,
Which will give your child release
From the ark of your embrace
That she may return with peace

Till she joins the elemental.
God himself now holds your daughter
Softly, too, by this most gentle
Rein of all, this drop of water.

VASSAR MILLER

Future Simple

What will be will:
Though day and night
Plan and prepare the fight,
Might out-mounting might.
What will be will.

What will be will:
Whichever way we try:
Welcome, postpone, deny:
Where? When? What?
Who? How? Why?
What will be will.

What will be will,
Far though we strain to see
Beyond mere you and me,
It's here our care will be
And still be, still.

I. A. RICHARDS

Without a Speaking Tongue

Without a speaking tongue time would stand still.
The cups of memory would wait to fill.
Bread would be broken without prayer.
No thought, no cry would find its sayer.
All lips would burn in unfinished desire
And flames would thirst for want of fire.

WALTER SORELL

Resurrection

Men, like leaves, are winnowed in a
    train
Of winds and waterings, and are the
    chance
Florescence of a moment, the advance
Form of an Autumn fire and of the
    wane
That bows to death in Winter. They are
    grain
That casually ripens on the lance,
Then withers, mocking its own arro-
    gance,
Under the rippled impact of the rain.
Yet these, the withered ones, make very
    meal
Of marvel: pounded by the angry thrust
Of all the pain, the passion and the toil
That lingers in their living from the
    soil,
They are not crushed!-though boundenly they steal,
No man astonished, down into the dust.

WILLIAM HENRY FANNING

Under Oaks

In a hushed, tremendous descent
Like the banishment of iron and glass
From heaven to earth in confusion,
The rain falls,

And the tree, in every leaf,
Huddles, to be nearer your head.
Instinctively you bow
As in a church
Flung down on you in panic from a cloud.
Perhaps it is here the lightning comes
To think of the sky's imprint
And the chosen tree.
At this thought you lift your head
And touch the tree yourself.
From your finger leaps no fire
Or holy mark,

But into you, out of the earth,
Flows enormous pride and daring
And the huge and joyous denial

Of the lightning
That has chosen, and stood alone
In a cloud of water, thinking
Of heaven emblazoned in wood, and said
Not now, not yet.

JAMES DICKEY

PART II

PEOPLE AND PORTRAITS

Mrs. Arbuthnot

Mrs. Arbuthnot was a poet
A poet of high degree,
But her talent left her;
Now she lives at home by the sea.
In the mornings she washes up,
In the afternoons she sleeps,
Only in the evenings sometimes
For her lost talent she weeps,
Crying: I should write a poem,
Can I look a wave in the face
If I do not write a poem about a sea-wave,
Putting the words in place.
Mrs. Arbuthnot has died,
She has gone to heaven,
She is one with the heavenly combers now
And need not write about them,
Cry: She is a heavenly comber,
She runs with a comb of fire.
Nobody writes or wishes to
Who is one with their desire.

STEVIE SMITH

The Revolutionary

I was that youth. Now, from myself estranged,
After the revolution I was seeking,
I stop stone dead, to hear another speaking:
'Change nothing: you yourself must first be changed.'
I travelled seas and learnt to read a chart,
Knew how to navigate through dispossession
The hardest straits, yet wrote in my confessions:
'All triumph was resisted by the heart.'
Much evil and much good remain, and yet
The heart has no immaculate remedy.
Life, to be won, is won less easily;
The stars remind us: 'Your own eyes are set.'
Say of this patience that impatience gained:
'When others left their station, he remained.'

VERNON WATKINS

Vain Dream for John Clare

*Clare, John (1793–1864). The Northamptonshire peasant poet.
Wrote The Shepard's Calendar (1827), Rural Muse
(1835). Confined in a lunatic asylum.* THE READER'S
ENCYCLOPEDIA.

Oh, John Clare,
If only on some damp, dawn walk,
As you flustered frogs, froze misted quail,
Took happy care
To crush no kingcup, hedge no nesting hawk,
Delight in cranky caterpillar's trail—

You'd met me.
Stratagemmed with dew, I'd not have smiled,
But wreathing crowns of hawthorn, heightened blush
To make you see
My eyes, my lips, my yellow hair blown wild,
As fairly as convolvulus or thrush.

I would, John Clare,
Have crazed with artifice your rustic passion
Until you loved me more than fern or mouse;
Then, when heart's despair
Was what you fought, frog fled, the blood-root ashen,
Have sheltered you, at least, from such a house.

JOAN HUTTON

A Commemoration for the Physicist X

My friend awaited truth. It made me proud
To think of him, then tall, the sturdy jaw
Held firm against the wind, his figure bowed.

I liked to think his mind had come to flower
In pain and suffering. That was the flaw
In him, you see, that gave his presence power.

It made him real. The pain had sketched his face,
Its lines like those the Venetians blow in glass—
So wise, so crisp. And the slivers of disgrace

Were there—the scorn, the secret fear, the anger.
I like to think of these and could surpass
The bounds of envy, imagining pain the stronger

Of influences on him. Or then the pleasure
I got from simply knowing he had won—
That was the best. It gave his image measure.

For he had got his triumph; and, enraged,
Accepted its small fame, his labor done;
And suddenly his body's juices aged.

He grew, I felt, much taller, growing old
And, relinquishing, belittled the death that came—
His mind's good fury, abutment from the cold,

Protecting him as in high drapery.
That's how he died: all proud beyond all pain.
He took his leave—and left this memory.

PAUL OPPENHEIMER

Notes to the Life of Ovid

In *exsilio*, somewhere around Pontus
The old poet dreamed of Corinna.
Summer was past. Around the flickering lantern
Stray moths led their blind and barbarous dance,
The stray moths of Pontus that under his glance
Became the city's women and animals.

Animals is a hard word, he reflected
And smiled a little, being a cavalier.
A wind came. He forgot that he was smiling.

It was not a youthful, poetic mood
But it was autumn, deep enough for patience
And so he sat with still hands for a long time
Watching behind the dancers the figure of Corinna
Who might, perhaps, have moved in the same way.

ANDRAS HAMORI

Mozart

He never saw a tree, they say,
when he rode in his rumbling coach,
peg-seated and easy to lurch,
through the forests of Germany.
He sat with a pad on his knee
and braced himself, head and toe,
and sketched on his rocky way
four quartets and one symphony.

The birds all sang, as he passed,
and featured glissando, their wings;
brooks murmured their musical songs,
but on him, these nice metaphors lost.
No time! only time to be pressed
between measures, the genius too fast.
He made his decision, and placed
three eighth-notes behind a half-rest.

JANE MAYHALL

Dusk

My mother is looking down on my small brother
Who, sick a week, lay thin in a pale sleep.
Five years pass, ten,
A war came and is over,
But will the doctor ever arrive in time?

In those days any help seemed a long way off
And for all I know it never came at all.
Fifteen years, twenty,
Her face like a mask on the wall
And the wallpaper slowly fading into the dusk.

She would not eat her supper, refused the time,
Though all of us left home, even my brother.
But she is so steadfast
That nothing will ever change
And no good news can hurt her from the future.

LEONARD E. NATHAN

Old Woman in a Cage

She moves across the unlit hall to greet me,
Holding out her bony hand. I see her caught
Frail-faced and small between two window-bars
Beside her caged canaries. "*Figlio mio*, you are free."

Her flat, once part of a palace—crumbling, grey,
Defaced—is large and choked with furniture.
"And after thirty years with him, *O figlio mio* . . ."
Silently she looks at me, in blank dismay.

Showing me a Sixteenth Century pagan scene
Frescoed on the ceiling—young supple nymphs
Delighting in the nearness of a naked god,
She smiles, "O *figlio*, the scenes they've seen."

She gives me coffee in the morning, cognac-laced,
Watching as I drink. "*Figlio*, have you thought
Of the future, of age, the collapse of the years?"
At night I hear her whimpering, alone and lost.

In her shut cage of flesh, with her black dead,
Beneath her painted ceiling, she consoles herself—
Though inconsolably the small trapped bird of longing
In her beats its wings against the taunting blood.

CHRISTOPHER HAMPTON

Almost Ninety

The last time I kissed her
I held a thin sparrow
her bones were that hollow

Where did she get the juice to turn
her eyes, to laugh at her great grandson
singing her jingle bells?

Now for my little dry wren
a cardboard box could serve as nest.
Too frail for feathers, she took my kisses,

waving come back, come back again.

RUTH WHITMAN

Roethke

Why do we make these journeys,
Driving out at dawn, alone, toward a woods' edge?
On foot, we search through trees for the brook's
Sound, a stone to sit on and contemplate
Water rushing over rocks. The morning haze
Hangs on the pines and maples,
Warblers sing and a toad glints in sunlight.

For what purpose these journeys,
Except to know the limits of a word, a poem.
Leaving one world, we enter another
Ready to notice differences—
Of sunlight on a man, a leaf, a toad,
Or differences between the poet and the man.

Word comes that a student is killed,
A pink, slender girl thrown by an errant horse,
The bird heart crushed, the spirit stilled.
That was your finest moment, knowing a poet's place,
When to speak, what to say, when to stop.
It was the father and lover in you.

HOWARD HEALY

In Memory of Robinson Jeffers

If he could have looked ahead
and found the unusual weather:
snow, rarest from clouds in our
mild winters, falling outside his
windows, over Point Lobos and the
coast range mountains, he might have
chosen the day he died as a good time
to leave: the quietest heart of winter
anyone here remembers, the unheard
and unheard of snow; the strange white
landscape. In that silence he was as safe
as the birds and beasts in his poems,
a sanctuary from his own kind where
he could keep, immaculate, his own
identity, and leave his beloved coast
at last and leave, save in his poems,
no trace, no trace at all.

ERIC BARKER

Mad Actor

His memory control stop being broken
His brain releases all it once confined.
All stored for speaking there is now respoken
Quotations are unquoting from his mind.

His earliest parts are interspersed among
Speeches from leads of a maturer year,
All uttered trippingly upon the tongue
In one soliloquy his whole career.

Hamlet's madness is real. He tells the tale
That nothing signifies. He is the player
That struts and frets, emotion at full scale,
Before an audience of empty air.

He takes an actor's dream part for his last,
Speaking as every member of the cast.

JAMES L. MONTAGUE

One Sort of Poet

Though he lift his voice in a great O
And his arms in a great Y
He shall not know
What his heart will cry
Till the fountain rise
In his columned throat
And lunge at the skies
Like a butting goat

And fall again from the tumid sky
In a rain of sound
Or a piercing sigh
On a fruitful ground.
Whatever spring
From the struck heart's womb
He can only sing
"Let it come! Let it come!"

A. J. M. SMITH

To A. E. Housman

Let now the willow weep no more
That wept within his mind,
But bear the long leaves that it bore,
Left for a while behind,
While he lies easy in a place
Where beds need little change,
And where the bedfellow to face
Shall not be lost nor strange.

Even to persons born as he,
Knowing too much to know,
Except that there is Spring to see
And blossoms hung like snow;
And not so very much to say,
Save in the saying well;
There comes an uneventful day
With nothing left to tell.

WITTER BYNNER

The Beekeeper

An old man, whose flannel undershirt
is buttoned through the frosty hairs
of his chest, shuffles among hives
and trembles his fingers upon
the trays, withdrawing, placing.

As he works, he smokes his pipe
to numb his children into peace;
queens have eaten from his hands,
and he has fostered cities.

Now, when he squats, his knees crack
and his godlike vision blackens
like a storm cloud in the sun.
His wife has worried for years
about the bees that swarm drowsily
upon his ears and shoulders.
But he is intent only on his tasks
of small dimension, and even at nights
when he lies in sleep as dreamless
as stones, weeds or apple trees,
his fingers smell of honey.

JACK MATTHEWS

Eurasian Girl

There is no polemic between East and West
in that sweet and yet ivory firm face, no
cloud over the clear spring, nor darkest
current in the set of cross-cut agate.
She walks as wisely as the mandarins go

and in her hair the shadows in Saskia's dark hair
where her husband made brown the color of infinity.
Standing clear, where she is dark she is also fair
against the horizon of her lithe history.
Small wonder her eyes mirror the Amsterdam sky.

She holds her veil of hair across
her mouth to muse: if Vermeer had seen
her dulcet distant listening to the loss
of sound as a horse draws the scene
of morning landscape after him in the blue scheme

of Sunday morning, with oranges and kitten,
he might have painted her gold-flecked
in bed dark and fair amid the heavy linen
watching, with the air of hearing Mass,
her Sunday watcher and acolyte, her djin-djin.

ANTHONY KERRIGAN

Monk Begging, Kyoto

A basket over his head
hid whether he was young or old.
The wickerwork tilted back from his shoulder enough
for him to get a flute end in his mouth
and play music at the open front of the shop.
Where saucepans hung from the beams of the ceiling.
Hurrying cars and motorbikes
buried the archaic sounds of his music
learned in a cloistered hall edged by a veranda
overlooking gardens of moss and groves of bamboo.
When the shop owner, shivering in his padded robe,
put a coin on the held-out flowered fan, he bowed
and raised the flute again to hidden lips.
What dream of living on a holy mountain top
floats in the few notes like birds beside flowing water,
like birds on branches that are bare,
hunched and chirping in a bright winter?
Stalks that are icicles change to flower stems.
A piece of cut reed, with holes, can allow music to come
and save a human heart from indifference.

EDITH SHIFFERT

For Keats and the Florentine Night

The selfsame song? I'm far south from the dale
where you poured not in vain your warm despair,
printing your velvet words on future air
that we might know you as our nightingale.

The usignuolo's not as fine, they say,
yet he's nocturnal, shuns the Italian sun;
began at dark the fanfare and the run,
and bravely parried my black hours away,

as you, not born for death these hundred years,
have beat your sweet gong-full of English sounds
even across the sea to younger grounds,
even to western nights and wilder ears.

Song has no nation, grief no countryside.
Until light comes, I hear you at my side.

GERTA KENNEDY

The Emperor's Double

(*To my great-grandfather*)

Music and Tartar voices; horses; the kiss
Of wild mimosa; the long Cossack plain;
The cream and gilt of winter palaces;
River-beds big with brown alluvial rain;
Imperial counterfeit, through this land he goes,
The double of the double-eagle's lord,
Province and city, where the marshalled rows
Hide anarchies for freedom or reward.
The gunshot and the scuffle in the crowd
His English ear ignores; raising white glove
He passes for the Emperor; a shroud
Falls in the morgue on someone else's love.
He has none. Wife dead, only daughter lost,
An English landscape pulls him to retire.
He trots it through in dog-cart, the sole ghost
Of gun, the keeper's or the pheasanting squire.
So dies, at home, in bed: Danube remote,
Minaret town in Balkan mountain furled.
Till pistol-shots that never stained his coat
Split Sarajevo, wipe away a world.

ROBERT GITTINGS

T. S. Eliot

Eliot saw much, thought he saw more:
Hair-shirts as summer underwear
Showed forth that he, like Everyman, bore
More than almost every man could bear,
Yet quietly, in what he wore.
He was the poet's astronaut:
He voyaged backward into Donne
And outward to a still point, thought
To be beyond, though like, our Sun,
And far past, though not unlike, Nought.
Yet, thank his dance, his stillest point
Flew like a locus into seas
And through backyards, making conjoint
Sweet peas with apotheoses,
Big Muddy with all blood anoint.

THOMAS WHITBREAD

To the Portrait of an Unknown Man

Upon a high, unfriendly wall,
Above a hearth that others claim,
You look across the silent room
At those who do not know your name.
On wintry evenings when the snow
Lies deep on shadowed walk and lawn,
In Summer, when late, leveling suns
Seep through the shutters, thinly drawn,
On nights, through thick, conforming dark,
On early mornings, nickel-bright,
The mystery of your eyes remains,
Holding a last, inherent light
Against that distant day that knew
The flesh and blood that once was you.

This is the only link that lies
Between you and the years to be—
The last, lone courier stumbling on
Through dusks of dark eternity.
What secrets lie beyond your gaze
The curious mind can only guess;
The eyes that gleaned another age
Stare, out of time, at nothingness.
And yet, somehow, I seem to know
That in a dim shop, long ago,
Some heir, grown heedless of the past—
With penury and shame distraught—
Bartered for more immediate gold
This richness that the artist wrought.

Your eyes cry out against the deed
That brought you here, without a name,
To hang upon a stranger's wall,
An exile, in an antique frame,—

That sent you, aimless, through the world,
Striving to shape the lips upon
The little syllables that stand
Between you and oblivion.

ANDERSON M. SCRUGGS

Isabel Sparrow

Isabel Sparrow, who is she?
Brought up in conversation and put down,
A thin sweet woman flashed upon the air
And vanished through the haze of a lost town.

Was it a hundred years or two she walked
In her tidy leather shoes?
Did she find love, bear children? Questions press
Hard to my heart, leaving a curious bruise.

For no one can tell, no one remembers or wonders
Or even is certain why
Her name came up, like a drifting leaf, to be spoken
And casually passed by.

Isabel Sparrow, fate grants us no quarter,
Flashes your faint blue smile, and then no more.
It is enough—at night I hear the seawind
Blowing and blowing through your vanished door.

MARY OLIVER

Portrait of a Certain Gentleman

This man's uncertain; he's afraid
To make a choice which, being made,
He must abide by, bad or good,
So he'd avoid it, if he could.

He'd like to hide away, to run
Out of reality's broad sun
Into a cave, a hole, a crack
In earth's kind substance. He'd go back

To what he fancies was secure,
The state of childhood, which was sure,
Since he was told what he must do.
That world's grown up, the man has too.

Poor child, poor man, there's no escape
From what is termed your adult shape,
This form which you attain at last
Through such betrayals in the past.

Nor God nor man will tell you now
What you must do, or when, or how—
There's no retreat that may be won to,
No one except yourself to run to.

SARA HENDERSON HAY

Evangel

As though the streets were all downhill
he lunges against the crowds,
clutching the Book,
his glare a pointed lance,
bearing no banner but his rage.
Police ignore him; shoppers stare.
Stenographers, eleven stories up,
turn to the window at his shout,
hearing their names.
Prophet or knight
or avatar,
this is his kingdom, plainly marked.
Who anointed him, or from what stone
he drew his sword,
are questions lost within his cry.
Slayer of dragons,
hawker of heaven,
he hurls against our pride
the only litany he knows.
What souls he saves we cannot
guess;
perhaps his own.

JEAN BURDEN

Diary of a Nondescript

I have taken the lash of today like a
      cowed animal:
    Being racket-wise, I have passed the
      poor in the street;
I have stood at the foot of a desk like
      a stooped numeral,
    Divided, multiplied, junked—but a man
      must eat;
I have said no! no! no! to Beauty
      when she touched my arm in the
      street.

I have sat in the house of my friend,
      too weak for exhorting him;
    I have taken the taunt of my enemy
      into my breast,
Too tired to conquer him, either by love
      or by hurting him;
    I have looked at the evening papers,
      and smoked, and undressed—
    I have seen the headlines in the papers;
      I have dreamed of the Isles of the
      Blest.

GARRETT OPPENHEIM

Balzac

Poor Balzac, relegated to a back room,
playing host to cobwebs on your startled face.
Relax. Nothing can ever mar your greatness
nor turn your sensuousness to stone.

DARCY GOTTLIEB

Marcel Proust

His childhood he gave to a public which had none,
And then withdrawing to a cork-lined room,
Lived ever after. . . . On his pages sprawl
Sentences like vine leaves on the wall
Of some well-weathered ruin where the sun
Picks out the childlike letters on a tomb.

WILLIAM JAY SMITH

Island Cook

Hers was a world of chowders, stews,
Bay leaf and butter-sweet clouds of steam
Scenting the curtains, glazing beams
Of her slant-walled kitchen pitched to view
A tide-shaken landing lashed to the knees
Of granite cliffs, stained to their caps
With the ocean's blood. No winter snapped
Her mind's great wish to draw the sea
Into the fragrant mists of this room
Where it might pound the shores of her heart,
Clinging to the memory of a seaman's heart,
Drifting through doors of his ocean tomb,
And surrender up some button of bone,
Some wax of his ear, some weed of his brain—
Something to bury in afternoon rain
When kitchens are lighted, when knives are honed.

WILLIAM GOODREAU

The Geranium Man

Observe, from his trunk upwards,
his shirt blossom out wild as spring;
hear the insensible words,
the nasal voice with which he sings:
the world's lover, see him bow
to strangers (God, anything
and nothing are significant!),
this admirable innocent,
holy as a Hindu cow.

The budgerigar bells, the long
hair, this geranium man in his pot,
what he sings is not a song
and what he thinks is not a thought.
Blown-up poster gestures for speech
(oh but his metaphysics cannot
bear words), he applauds purities
whose own ecstasy lies
in the real being out of reach.

ZULFIKAR GHOSE

Abstract Painter in Spring

My woods, obscurely dim, will shelter
spirit, song and essence—seldom
flowers to which names are to be fused,

birds to which feathers may be fixed.
Abstraction, for me, is not a name
for a style but a process of thought by which

all flowers, all birds may spring to life:
herb Robert, frail beside the path,
the yellow-billed cuckoo rarely glimpsed,

waxwing and appleblossom.
                              So here
my brush should leave a darker passage;
the glossy pigment, upswept, evoke
the sense of eagles high on a snag
above the implausible nest, their awesome
providence lifting only now

as the two great birds, alarmed,
fly off to the nearer woods, slow-moving,
silent, purposely driving as paint.

ROSAMOND HAAS

Potato Digger

All day along potato hills, this woman
Moved with an ancient rhythm in her blood;
All day she leaned above the mystery
Of fertile earth that gives man stronger food
Than meets the body's hunger, and her soul
Is nourished now by wonder old as breath.
She rises from the furrows, and her feet
Press slowly on the passionate world beneath.
This woman cannot stand erect. All day
Her body bowed above the ground; the pull
Of the sun-hot field still draws her shoulders downward.
She has felt out the warm fruit beautiful
As flesh, and left the earthy heaps behind.
Her hands are dark with soil, her knees are bent
Outward, her body smells of loam and sun,
Her eyes are evening-colored and content.

FRANCES FROST

The Hunchback

Within the house of mirrors
amazedly he sits
and studies in the mirrors
how well his hunchback fits.

He picks up his book of riddles
and tumbles his game of blocks.
How many tears in an onion?
How many springs in clocks?

Flies turn to bones of amber
when the spider spins itself,
and he sighs into cobwebs
and the clock sighs on the shelf.

He treads his growing shadow,
and walks the endless round
along the edge of the mirror sea
where a hunchless ghost lies drowned.

ROBERT FRIEND

Table D'Hote

While Mr. Charleston, the maître d'hôtel,
is boning the Dover sole,
he talks of Cornwall
and Penzance where he was born.
In the blue flame of the alcohol lamp
under the drawn butter
he sees violets,
the smell of them weighted with the foggy mornings
he went to school along the cliffs.
He remembers the boatloads of daffodils
coming in from the Scilly Isles
over the sunken land of Lyonesse.
But most particularly he remembers
how the herring fleet tacked out of Long Rock,
brown sails triangulating the sunset,
and how their masthead lanterns glinted
over the chop of dusk,
the not-quite-dark horizon glimmering
with points of light
and Land's End extending infinitely, infinitely
into the blue-black sea.
Suddenly, that is why he is here,
years away,
boning the Dover sole.

RICHARD CURRY ESLER

Francis Parkman

(Returning from the Oregon Trail)

Unsteady in the saddle,
    He visited the Sioux,
Observing through a haze
    The life that he could use.

It wasn't quite the atmosphere
    For one to keep his calm in,
Who was no noble savage,
    But a noble Brahmin.

Something in the wilderness
    Just put him off his ease;
Something like his breeding
    Assailed him in the knees.

Returning to the settlements,
    And plainly feeling better,
He acted then the veteran
    And scrawled a virile letter.

No Lochinvar who loomed
    Heroic from the west,
He gravitated toward the east
    To where he flourished best—

At home with pen and paper,
    Secure of board and bed,
And Boston exorcising
    His prairie-haunted head.

ERNEST KROLL

Wilbur's Garden

Is situated at the foot of Chocorua,
Laid out in a square.
Staked chickenwire prevents the deer.
Early asparagus, rhubarbs are looking around.

Wilbur walks bent over.
His body has sucked up rheumatism like a chestnut.
He chuckles the asparagus out of the ground.
He is god out of a piece of hard fruit
Saying nothing,
Smells old; like a shed, a barrel, like the promise of mold.

WALTER CLARK

Antique

Hands we sign our names with touch this trinket,
And eyes we search with find this dusty chair;
You were never without this ring and this locket;
These deserted brushes worked your hair.

This torn book aroused your scarce laughter,
And these black dresses made your face austere;
But you had charm, and that was almost beauty.
Things you kept so secret still are here.

Hands we write our names with hold this paper,
And eyes we search with read that worthless vow
That left you always strong, aloof, and cautious.
Things you loved, we use and know not how.

JOHN STEVENS WADE

Night School

What draws you here at night, gray-headed man,
    Whose back is bent as by a weight of stone?
Stoop-shouldered woman, what strange magic can
    With mystic ritual for life atone?
The balm you find in printed books, in talk,
    Has little might beyond the moment's use;
It is impermanent as teacher's chalk,
    As powerless as tears against abuse.
And yet you know within this crowded room
    A peace as sacred as the Pilgrims knew
Who crossed the sands to find a refuge, whom
    Pillars of fire and light companioned too,
The desert momently produces manna
And choirs of penciled scripts proclaim hosanna.

ELIAS LIEBERMAN

You Give Me Sappho

You give me Sappho and the wind-blown hills
Fringed with blue crocus nodding to the sea
At Mytelene; all her subtle skills
Of lyric beauty you bequeath to me
In soft lip-magic from some happy store
Of mystery that veils you like a nun.
The moon-drenched, placid nights I've hungered for—
Within your eyes' blue dreaming are begun.

When I have slipped from out your loving, then
Be tender, for beneath love's portico
I warmed my heart against your spirit when
There was no other human place to go;
And come to claim me down irrelevant years,
A slim madonna haunting me with tears.

SISTER M. THERESE

· 158 ·

For Marian Anderson

Who will say that music is all we've heard?
Hushed in halls where song by song displayed,
In reaches of accurate ease, the incredibly hard,
But deeply sweet, revelations our hopes implied,
Could even the deaf to grace not sense—if ever—
Among the soulful timbres so richly shared
The quiet bond whose life-giving never is over?
Where has that concert-tide on silence shored?

For where are farewells spoken? Backstage, or by trains,
Stunned with pleasure, who have heard the Word,
And lost in babble's waking second trance
Of translating each other's inspired reward,
We know by our unstrangered sympathies
Tomorrow the world will think and feel like this.

FREDERICK BOCK

Statue in a Blizzard

(*Greeley Square*)

Fame should not be personified
In the rude solitude of stone
And then exposed to every weather of the world:
Think of that firebrand, Horace Greeley, anonymous in snow,
    Sitting there speechless on his pedestal
    All through this polar night alone.

RUTH DOUGLAS KEENER

A Ride in a Blue Chevy from Alum Cave Trail to Newfound Gap

goin' hikin'?
git in!

o the Smokies are ok but me
I go for Theosophy,
higher things, Hindu-type philosophy,
none of this licker and sex, I
like it
on what we call the astral plane,
I reckon I get more i-thridral
by the hour

buddy, you won't believe this but
how old you reckon the earth is?
the earth is
precisely 156 trillion years old—
I got this book from headquarters in
Wheaton, Illinois
says it is!

I'll tell you somethin' else:
there are exactly 144 kinds of people on earth—
12 signs and the signs change
every two hours,
that's 144, I'm Scorpio,
with Mars over the water

here's somethin' else innerestin':
back 18 million years
people was only one sex, one sex only . . .
I'd like to explain that,
it's right here in this pamphlet,
50 cents . . .

never married, lived with my mother in Ohio,
she died, I'm over in Oak Ridge
in a machine shop, say,
what kind of place
is Denver?
think I'll sell this car, go to Denver,
set up a Center . . .

name's Davis,
what's yours?

                    JONATHAN WILLIAMS

Bran

Like Aristaeus, seeking the secret of the bees,
He haunts the fog-embellished shore,
His leather apron falls about his knees,
He listens to the wind's lugubrious snore
And traces and retraces all his steps
Among the rocks, beside the lobster pools—
From shining, opaque stone he chips
His useless and outmoded tools
And sits beside the tarn and waits
And listens for the mermaid's song—
For time is fog, he knows no dates—
Eternity to him is merely long
And counted by the billows' metronome
Or by the wildly whirling rain—
And he will make the rocks his home
Till all the other gods return again.

GEORGE H. MOORSE

OF POETRY,
ART, AND ARTISTS

To Calliope

Permit me here a simple brief aside,
    Calliope,
You who have shown such patience with my pride
    And obstinacy:

Am I not loyal to you? I say no less
    Than is to say;
If more, only from angry-heartedness,
    Not for display.

But you know, I know, and you know I know
    My principal curse:
Shame at the mounting dues I have come to owe
    A devil of verse,

Who caught me young, ingenuous and uncouth,
    Prompting me how
To evade the patent clumsiness of truth—
    Which I do now.

No: nothing reads so fresh as I first thought,
    Or as you could wish—
Yet must I, when far worse is eagerly bought,
    Cry stinking fish?

ROBERT GRAVES

The Wonder Shell

(Thatcheria mirabilis)

Under museum glass it is remote
as architecture;
a treasure, not a creature.
The wonder is, alive below Japan
a particle of flesh
clung to a spur of bone
against the pressure of the sea, and flared
a spiral skeleton.
The animal within,
according to the rhythm of its kind,
spun out its porcelain
and died, defined.
We, more inward in our nature, trace
of our own spiral motion
as durable a sign
that, for a little time, we too displace
a portion of an ocean.
Seekers on the shore
who never know the beauty of our bones,
and find our art remote,
will sense what animal
made this, to die defined,
preserving wonder whole
as treasure from a far more perilous sea.

BARBARA D. HOLENDER

The Death of Hoelderlin

(suffered with madness from his thirty-seventh until his seventy-third year, when he died)

He weakened outwardly. His skin
Stayed firm but loose feathers of his hair
Flattened where the firm had been
So, fondling these, he felt he weakened there.

He saw then something stern and strange,
A bracelet of darkness, clasping him.
Stiffly he perceived a change:
A world outside his eyes was falling dim.

We hear him grow hysterical
That world releasing him, and crypts of verse
Open and hide his shriveled skull . . .

We know he suffered, but see his art rehearse
The peace that filled him when his grave was full.

PAUL OPPENHEIMER

To the Poets of India

I read poems taken from old Indian tongues
Bengali, Urdu, Hindi, Telugu, Kannada
"Engraved with lines of agony"
Or with the "irrepressible desire to utter Omkar"
The name of God
And it seemed of me they were speaking.
When their tears fell, they poured out my anguish,
Far glories were mine on the Punjabi hills,
In the eyes of their women I saw the passion too.

Strange images were used. I do not know
"The thin branches of siris, anlaki, bocul and neen,"
Nor how "A baby vulture cries out in a banyan,"
But the image of the image is the same.
Where I sit now, against this Canadian sky,
Branches of maple and of elm are thin,
A cry goes up in the night,
And over in Caughnawaga
The band of Iroquois broods on what is lost
As Mohammed Iqbal stood in Sicily
And wept Granada's lovely rise, and fall.

F. R. SCOTT

The Thin Man, a Sculpture

Tall and thin,
a reed for winds to play,
he stands
and fingers final bone.
For flesh to fall away
the moment of decay
need never come,
the essence numb
from word and stone
and senses that betray.
He stands alone,
the minimum of self,
all channels of the felt
destroyed, unknown.
He climbs the steep
catastrophe of bone
toward the deep
impenetrable sky
and fails to die.

GEORGE MURRAY

A Bright Day

At times I see it, present
As a bright day, or a hill,
The only way of saying something
Calmly (and clearly) as possible.

Not the accumulated richness
Of an old historical language—
That musk-deep odour
But a slow exactness

That recreates the experience
By ritualising its details—
The colour of the curtain,
The width of the table—

Till all takes on a witch-bright glow
And even the clock on the mantelpiece
Moves its hands in a fierce delight
Of so, and so, and so.

JOHN MONTAGUE

Not a Tree

An oaktree cannot be mistaken,
By growing it climbs up to heaven;
Since for a man, unlike a tree,
Knowledge is growth, maturity
Is never an assured success
But what ten decades may bypass.
No bough or blemish, leaf or frond
Their destiny did not intend,
As each year by one wooden ring
Trees move towards their perishing;
But you and I must conjure out
Volition from a buried root,
And, for ourselves, discover where
We have to go and who we are,
Or at long last lean down to enter,
Ungrown, the lenses of the winter.
Since of mortality stripped bare,
I would not be, still unaware
Of what it is the life intends
That walks my feet and grips my hands,
Or through death's door be lugged like trash,
An adult only in the flesh,
Though, mandrake-like, my root is broken
And always I must be mistaken,
To the compulsion of that root
I go again, to ravel out
One stem from forked duplicity,
Because a man is not a tree.

THOMAS BLACKBURN

The Studio

She came bringing unlikely bloom,
stepping long-limbed lightly,
almond blossoms for the room,
and gazed in the mirror faintly.
In the mirror, cans of paint,
Alizarin red and cerulean blue,
made a background fast and faint
for the portrait the branches drew.
When she turned her profile stayed,
the limbs of almond wheeled:
the glass at being woman played
and she all art revealed.

ANTHONY KERRIGAN

Abstract Painter

He fell into blue
as the sirens blinded.
His love of blue
was the blue apron
of the nurse who loved him.

He jumped headstrong
into palest green, his
blood spurting.

Beyond his elbow
is not the horizon
nor night's mulberry.
It's the smell of black oblongs
blended with brown—
they are moving gently
into crash and crisis
into clash and clamor
of Grecian urns sharding.

GERTA KENNEDY

Six Lines Unheard

Six decent lines can make a man immortal
Said Ezra Pound. But what if, kicking/pounding at a portal

No one hears, let alone answers his six pleas,
Or six curses set in metric similes,

Excepting dogs and children? "Listen! Let me in!"
Gets nothing but a blackened fist, and bruising shin?

DIANA DER HOVANESSIAN

La Creazione Degli Animali

Here that old humpback, Tintoretto, tells
Of six days' labor out of Genesis:
Swift from the bowstring of two little trees
Come swans, astonished basilisks and whales,
Amazed flamingos, moles and dragonflies
To make their lifelong helpless marriages;
Time is a place at last; dumb wonder wells
From the cracked ribs of heaven's gate and hell's.

The patriarch in that vicinity
Of bubble seas and eggshell esplanades
Mutters his thunder like a cloud. And yet
Much smaller issues line the palm of God's
Charged hand: a dog laps water, a rabbit sits
Grazing the footprint of divinity.

JOHN MALCOLM BRINNIN

The Honeybee

Just now a honeybee
Put me in mind of him
By furiously chasing me,
Convinced I had to be stung
For aspiring to honeysuckle
And honey on my tongue.

Pindar, when he was young,
Was set upon by a swarm
Of honeybees. Black as a cloud
Before a summer storm
They gathered, a threatening mass,
And settled on his lips

As he lay in the grass,
And in multitudes they clung.
But the honey they left behind
Put dithyrambs in his mouth,
Panegyrics came to his mind,
And he spoke with a honeytongue.

HELEN BEVINGTON

Mural of Borodino

Once gold and vermilion on white plaster,
Those grand armies are worn down and peeled back
From walls grown gray as snow under cracked bones
Whose gray marrow seeped out long ago.
Poor scarecrows, they are dragging home
Black iron and banners wrapped in snow.
Tattered victory, defeat; one cannot tell.
Soiled wall and men, soiled snow.
Pain, a little egg yolk, a little gold leaf
On brilliant new white plaster, will revive
Their vivid tale, and paint for our delectation
One more vermilion drop of gore—one fresh heroic war.

LUCILE ADLER

Spindle

Song is a violence
of icicles and
    windy trees:

rising it catches up
indifferent
    cellophane, loose

leaves, all mobiles
into an organized whirl
    relating scrap

to scrap in a round
fury: violence
    brocades

the rocks with hard silver
of sea water and
    makes the tree

show the power of its
holding on: a
    violence to make
    that can destroy.

A. R. AMMONS

El Greco

Flame-like limbs, tortured green
In your merciless longing I burn,
Fire of the rootless who turn
Blindly to reach for the unseen,
To touch the hidden side
Of clouds where all the tempests meet—
Blood dropping from the heart of Crete
Across Toledo's cruel pride.

Behind that feast of agony I feel
Rigid the saints on dome and wall
Who watch a praying Empire fall,
A Muslem-broken world clenched to the wheel.
In this bruised light, this lust
Of twisted flesh that finds no rest
Byzantium is grappling with the West
To mend the broken trust.

And all the lonely flesh burns in that fire,
Hung on a tree naked of branch and leaf,
A rugged gesture of grief
Wrenching faith from the venter of desire;
Until nails crushing the warped feet and palms,
The yellow drops of blood,
Shiver like blossoms on the bitter wood
And swallows flood the stretching cross's arms.

C. A. TRYPANIS

Song

Old friends
when I was young
you laughed with my tongue
but when I sang
for forty years
you hid in your ears
hardly a greeting

I was
being poor
termed difficult
tho I attracted a cult
of leeches
and they signed love
and drank its cordials
always for giving
when they were receiving
they presumed
an infinite forgiveness

With my weak eyes
I did not see
assumed a bit
of infinite myself
arrogating hypocrisy
to no heart
but stupidity

LOUIS ZUKOFSKY

Repeated in Thin Gold

Remembering one day when your wide
      eyes
Opened to startle me for the first time,
Undedicated moment, did the tree
That bears futurity burst into bloom
With lovelier flowers than we could
      realize?

The roar, the thunder of the barbaric
      city,
Thunder that poured its heat in heart,
      in head
Grew mild with tenderness and soft
      with pity,
What happy rumor woke the unhappy
      dead?

The sacred moment fades, but thought
      is long:
Oh, unbelievable, believe, say you be-
      lieve
Only in miracles, only in what comes
      to pass
In the dark midnight when the lost
      souls grieve
And the long twilight hides the Sum-
      mer grass.

That which is lost is found, the tenuous
      beauty snared,
The fine, the golden note caught and
      repeated:
Oh, how it rings on the ear, wild-sweet,
      round and completed.

MARYA ZATURENSKA

The Prisoner—
Galleria Dell'Academia

His art—the medium at war with craft:
The torso's tensile twist against the rock,
One arm around the canted head bent daft,
The other plunging down to fuse the shock.
Had thus explored the stone's complexity
Of mass in space for motion unrestrained
Except by form to set whatever free
The brutal stolid shapelessness contained.
So tempted matter's gross tenacity—
Now half-released the torso struggles still
To foil the stone's ingenuous deceit
As if escape could be an act of will—
Then finished it and left it incomplete.

IRWIN STARK

The Flowering Past

There is no poetry when you live there.
Those stones are yours, those noises are your mind,
The forging thunderous trams and streets that bind
You to the dreamed-of bar where sits despair
Are trams and streets: poetry is otherwise.
The cinema fronts and shops once left behind
And mourned, are mourned no more. Strangely unkind
Seem all new landmarks of the now and here.

But move you toward New Zealand or the Pole,
Those stones will blossom and the noises sing,
And trams will wheedle to the sleeping child
That never rests, whose ship will always roll,
That never can come home, but yet must bring
Strange trophies back to Ilium, and wild.

MALCOLM LOWRY

Tonight the Pacifist Moon

Tonight the pacifist moon was hit by a bomb.
Amidst the debris of dreams, the white dust,
I stood in a kind of cosmic comical calm,
Snowman-silly, frozen in that gust.
Then Ariosto came, pocked with a grin,
And Leopardi weeping and Shelley flying,
And Keats—Endymion's consumptive twin,
And Jules Laforgue—moon-monocled and sighing.
A harmless horde of poets, lovers, loons
Circled round me in a Maypole whirl
Singing cracked and out-of-fashion tunes
Giddying me as the skirts of a wild girl.
Then I looked up and where the moon had been
A black relentless tunnel sucked me in.

SIDNEY ALEXANDER

THE ANIMAL KINGDOM,
AND FABULOUS GARDENS

Blow Fish

Standing in silence,
we watch.
Past shame or shock,
his black eyes, aghast
at having failed to beat
the world at its own game,
wrinkle like early ice
on puddle-cups of grief.
His bone-breaker mouth
bites hard and lipless on the fact
of this dry, hot end on rock.
His fat sides heave.
With groan and gasp,
he belches brine.
His bowels relax.
At last, each barbed spike
bends back.
In silence, and standing,
we watch.

A. KIRBY CONGDON

The Trout

The water my prison shatters in a prism
As I leap alone the dying falls,
Cruel gasps of air, the musical chasm
Intrigue me with their broken intervals.

Deep in the noon of motionless canals
I dreamt away my pale reality
Till stirred by Her immortal voice Who calls
To the heights of the mountains and the depths of the sea.

I lean on air as prisoners on time
Not to let them down, my impetus
Only to the second hand sublime,
From every point of view ridiculous,

To climb the stair of stone where I was spawned,
Where ponds are oceans and the rapids give
Foretaste of the unbreathable beyond
I try, I fall, I wriggle loose, I live

Drop by drop against the stream I am,
And in death's little cataract belong
Like Tristan to the torrent and the dam,
Liquid chamber music and still current song,

As I was laid upon the deep sea floor,
Part of the faded pattern of the carpet,
Or split like the sperm the kissing fish ignore
Held in each other's scales as in a net,

Yes I exist, a memory in man
And beast and bird, a universal wish
For the watery world where life began
And your angelic avatar the fish:

Ambitious, ghastly, with protuberant eyes,
Or suspended like a living bathysphere.
I negotiate the steps of paradise
Leaping to measures that I cannot hear.

DARYL HINE

Fish-eye

The flounder, born erect, perversely turns
   Upon one side, and yet the lower eye,
Buried against the bottom, still discerns
   The light that filters dimly from the sky.

This mindless orb is magically unmoored
   And, prompted by a deep instinctive shove,
Moves like a pilgrim, till it has abjured
   The nether dark, and shared the glow above.

The human animal sees right and wrong
   With eyes that from uncompromising places
Often confuse the two, and thus prolong
   The moral crisis that the owner faces.

A man, beset by such a conflict, wishes
He had an eye as sure as this flat fish's.

MILTON BRACKER

The Wood Frog

I came across my cousin,
sunning itself, and I presumed
on kinship with a touch. Like leaves,
joined in their camouflage with fox
and squirrel, an autumn russet,
it was a pulse of earth on earth;
with white neck fluttering, black eyes
steeper than lake water, black waters.
Then it let me pick it up
and put it down again—
so still and self-sufficient,
so far from me,
I gave up all presumption.

JOHN HAY

Water Snake

Sinuous among the reeds,
    At my careless tread
You freeze to utter stillness.
    Your onyx cameo head
Lifted, searching and aware
    Of alien intrusion
You lie, a reed among the reeds
    In serpentine illusion.

A charcoal shadow cleanly striped
    With yellow pale as sun
Slanted through cobalt-shaded pines,
    You and the bank are one.

You pause, and stare . . . then through the reeds
   You vanish like a dream
To write your wraithlike going
   In a ripple on the stream.

ETHEL JACOBSON

The Parrot Fish

The shadow of the little fishing launch
Discreetly, inch by inch,
Crept after us on its belly over
The reef's uneven floor.

The motor gasped out drowsy vapor.
Seconds went by before
Anyone thought to interpret
The jingling of Inez's bracelet.

Chalk-violet, olive, all veils and sequins, a
Priestess out of the next Old Testament extravaganza,
With round gold eyes and minuscule buck-teeth,
Up flaunted into death

The parrot fish. And for a full hour beat
Irregular, passionate
Tattoos from its casket lined with zinc.
Finally we understood, I think.

Ashore, the warm waves licked our feet.
One or two heavy chords the heat
Struck, set the white beach vibrating.
And throwing back its head the sea began to sing.

JAMES MERRILL

Where the Manatee Plays and the Manta Ray Flutters

How, as we peer into tanks at these lives,
eyed at each side, one four-eyed, some blind,
some toothless or tailless and some of a kind
with teeth neat as needles or fins that are knives,
many slug ugly, one butterfly beautiful—
bright orange, banded with luminous stripes—
fish that are small or appall by their shapes—
anemone, dreamflower, streaming with tentacle,
the suction-mooned octopus bunched up and pitiful,
irregular crabs in rectangular waters
where the manatee plays and the manta ray flutters,
how, now we clearly see, varied and plentiful,
forms from the depth of things, dare we explore
what crawled through the surface, and not fear a metaphor?

HAROLD WITT

Goldfish

The bearded goldfish move about the bowl
Waving disheveled rags of elegant fin
Languidly in the light; their mandarin
Manner of life, weary and cynical,

Rebukes the round world that has kept them in
Glass bubbles with a mythological
Decor of Rhineland castles on a shoal
Of pebbles pink and green. Like light in gin,

Viscous as ice first forming on a stream,
Their refined feathers fan them on to no
Remarkable purpose; they close their eyes
As, mouths reopening in new surprise
About their long imprisonment in O,
They cruise the ocean of an alien dream.

HOWARD NEMEROV

Beach Encounter

Volvox the sea roller slithers in the spent spume
spilling silver sand, a baby serpent hiss
sounding at the edges like the
silken sigh of time
folding on itself.
Volvox the planet jumper wavers
in the slime
molecular with mosses stained
black with outer space,
convoluted carelessly with green
gains and losses,
a mesodermal orphic eye with
lashes pulled awry
combing out the quasars and
comets on the fly:
Flotsam of the gods.

CHARLES A. WAGNER

From a Porthole in the Ice

Drawn upward from the glass-green element
Into a bright and pitiless air,
The pickerel thrashes on the white-blue ice.

Watery tiger, tricked from a weedy lair,
Rages till its liquid muscles, spent
Of swimming, lock within a vise.

Iridescent gold and green,
Darker patterns in a chain,
Run and link along mosaic scales.

Lacquered colors stretch their sheen
Where the rigid length is lain.

The gaping mouth's enameled nails
Clench around the bitter weather—
Lure and prey are grown together.

WILLIAM VINCENT SIELLER

A Gryphon Sighted in an Iowa Flyway

On Forney's Slough the million gather:
Geese of the Northering: blue, snow, Canadas,
Rising in feather-storms, instinct for the Arctic.
And under a dead elm, in talon-torn ground,
I saw him stalk, who seemed their protector.
Restless, segréant, lashing his tail,
Couchant, sparing all, never trod upon any;
Took to the air with the foremost, on eagle's wings,
Strange and ungainly dirigible shape.

He will not fly the riverway South, in our fall;
But has crossed the Circle, the Pole,
And gone down the other side of the world
Along flyways. At the Golden Horn,
Anna Comnena will remark to the Emperor;
The Assyrian tugs at his stovepipe beard;
Serfs shade their eyes in the Kingdom of Trinacria;
And Egypt rears monoliths.
Three weeks later, the dead elm
Has put forth a crown of new leaves.

N. G. WESTERFIELD

The Centaur Overheard

Once I lived with my brothers, images
Of what we know best and can best become.
What I might be I learned to tell in eyes
Which loved me. Voices formed my name,

Taught me its sound, released me from its dread.
Now they are all gone. When I prance, the sound
From dark caves where my hooves disturb the dead
Orders no other promise. Underground,

Streams urge their careless motion into air.
I stand by springs to drink. Their brimming poise
Repeats the selfish hope of who comes there.
But I do not look, move, or make a noise.

EDGAR BOWERS

Iguanas

The lizards sprawl on the sun-baked stones,
Their pearly eyes fixed on the stagnant pools
Of the slow-moving river.
Their rough-scaled skins
Gleam in the brilliant light
Like many colored jewels.

On cautious feet I silently approach
To see their rainbow beauty lying heaped
So carelessly,
When, like an iridescent sigh they disappear,
Leaving a flash of azure,
Green and purple
Over the stones and in the quivering air.

DAVID ATAMIAN

Roo

My dog, half whippet, lives to run.
Even in sleep his thin legs move
After some swift, invisible quarry;
And over the slopes of weed and sun
He churns for hours, racing with
Old bones or balls or puzzled friends,
Shaggy and matted, who wonder at
His flight, that never curves or ends.
From me, his mistress, he has learned
Nothing of running or of joy—
Only the sullen taste of love,
Which strange emotion makes him wild
And as afraid as any child
Of separations. Day by day
He wakes, complete, and speeds away,
Until, somewhere, he thinks of me . . .
That love is costly seems not strange;
But that its fabrics wrap and change
The patterns of a leaping thing
Leaves me in doubt, sometimes. My dog,
Half whippet, lives to leap and run,
And so he does—a narrow craft
Flowing above earth's weeded ways—
Until, somewhere, my image burns
Into his spirit; and he turns
A frantic circle to this place
That warms his heart, but kills the race.

MARY OLIVER

Time Out

The donkey sat down on the roadside
Suddenly, as though tired of carrying
His cross. There was a varnish
Of sweat on his coat, and a fly
On his left ear. The tinker
Beating him finally gave in,
Sat on the grass himself, prying
His coat for his pipe. The donkey
(not beautiful but more fragile
than any swan, with his small
front hooves folded under him)
Gathered enough courage to raise
That fearsome head, lip in a daisy,
As if to say—slowly, contentedly—
Yes, there is a virtue in movement,
But only in going so far, so fast,
Sucking the sweet grass of stubbornness.

JOHN MONTAGUE

The Tigress

The raging and the ravenous,
The nocturnal terror in gold,
Red-fire-coated, green-fire-eyed,
The fanged, the clawed, the frightful
    leaper.
Great-sinewed, silent walker,
Tyrant of all the timid, the implacable

Devil of slaughter, the she-demon
Matchless in fury, matchless love
Gives her whelps in the wildernesses.
Gleaning the smears of slaughter
From her jaws with tongue and forearm,
She licks her young and suckles them
Delicately as a doe:
She blood-glutted is the angel
To their blindness, she is minister
Between life and these feeble young
In barren places, where no help is.

Or man-imprisoned often disdaining
To rear her royal brood, though cheated
Into bearing, she abandons
All at birth, and bids them die.
Utter love and utter hatred
Cannot compromise: she gives
Her whole being to their being
Or rejects them into death.

No thought intervenes; her justice
Is not mind-perverted: O tigress,
Royal mother without pity.
Could but one thought arise within
That greatly sculptured skull, behind
Those phosphorous eyes compunction
    burn.
Well might it be a thought for many
Men through the mother mind-betrayed,
No beast so hapless as a man.

RUTH PITTER

To a Mole

Go burrow in your hole,
My quite self-centered mole,
And you will never see
Sorrow or agony;
Keep safely hidden there
And you will have no care
Within the Stygian gloom
Of one small earthen room.
But keep this in your mind:
You, my dear mole, are blind
While those who have clear eyes
Must face life otherwise.

LOUISE DARCY

The Fawn

Lift up your head. Stop blood and breath.
Stare, shy one, from the familiar shade
Of forest, beyond which lies death,
And the live fury men have made.

Look how the grass moves, where it should
Be still this windless morning. Look!
Something is crouching there where stood
A bronze-leafed alder and a brook.

O wary one, why not go flying
Before you know? Why do you pause,
One foot lifted and one foot trying
The twig-strewn turf of leaves and straws?

It is I that bar your wide-eyed way.
I stalk the secret heart you bear.
Your nostrils know me, yet you stay
Tasting the cold, man-scented air.

Will you, if I am still and calm,
Come closer, suffer me to rise
And, holding up a weaponless palm,
Show you the fawn within my eyes?

RAYMOND HOLDEN

The Fox

I had to shoot a fox today. If he
Had been full-grown and healthy in his hate,
Or flung his fury headlong into me
As my hand tripped the latch that swung the gate
Of death to let him in, I might be proud
That he lies cold beneath the winter stars.
But he was thin and pitiful, and cowed
To see me standing fixed among my scars
With him as my revenge. In his pale eyes
(And this is what I hated most, I think)
Was neither light nor cunning. Too late wise
In knowing even to this ultimate brink
I favored him, I fired—nor could foresee
His dying with such inexorable dignity.

EDSEL FORD

The Chipmunk

He throws
his limited rug of stripes like a flash
over the pine needles. He goes
sampling the earth with quick paws:
bark, acorn-cup skoals, tamarack cones
guttered behind a log, sections
of phoebe shadow, the track
of field theory in sawdust.
He is a sawdust drunk
sliding belly-down through the dry-surfaced
litter left by the woodpile, swimming in
an aeon of oaks. Stone walls give him
accessible caves. He runs over them
faster than vision. Illusion
is less quick than he is and even sun
burns less than the stripes of his leaps
traveling between the stillnesses
of boulder and cucumber.
He sits tranced, eyes wide open
in attentive slumber—a leaf falls,
and he vanishes.

MILLEN BRAND

Camel

Though come down in the world to pulling a cart
Piled high as a house-top, camel, your gait
Proclaims, proclaims, proclaims the aristocrat.

Though your knees, like a clown's, wear bells that clash
Whenever your cushion-feet cuff the street,
A greater clown behind you swings the lash

Over your backside. History and he
Are unacquainted. From your ancestors
You have inherited history:

Philosophy becomes you like your hump:
Nobility speaks louder than these sores
And bells and the sweat on your angular rump.

I have seen your nostrils flare to a wind
Born nowhere in the port or festering slums,
But in the wastes beyond the wastes of Sind.

Heavily falls the lash. You neither turn
Nor flinch, but hooded in your eye there comes
A glint of snows above Baluchistan.

JON STALLWORTHY

The Fox

Incursive on the frozen snow,
Wary blaze in vulpine eyes,
Islanded in solitude,
The fox in moonlight on the rise
Kept his stance as I my own,
Chaos in him as in me,
Shut in the inviolate
Aorta, burning icily.

Malice in him; yet he knew
I too with infected will
Had set my trap, a stratagem
As secretive as his own skill;
The semblance of his evil, mine;
Mine as his; when in the numb
Absolute of silence, he
Disappeared as he had come.

I. L. SALOMON

The Albatross

Her I pursued across the Southern Sea,
My offering a snowy wake,
Myself, or the ship's company;

And I would see her at each break of day
Glide past me at my shoulder height,
Her wingtip just one strake away.

Although she would not take the lure
I fancied in her quiet, brown eye
An understanding, subtle & demure,

That such an ill-assorted pair must face
A separation worse than loneliness;
No sea is mine, no land her resting-place.

JOHN BIRAM

Owl

The cat-eyed owl, although so fierce
at night with kittens and with mice

in daylight may be mobbed
by flocks of little birds, and in
the market-place, be robbed

of all its dignity and wisdom
by children, market-women, and malingering men

who hoot at it and mocking its myopic
eye, shout 'Look!
Look at it now, he hangs his head in

shame.' This never happens to the eagle
or the nightingale.

EDWARD BRATHWAITE

The Bat

By day the bat is cousin to the mouse,
He likes the attic of an aging house.

His fingers make a hat about his head.
All flesh and blood with slower pulse is dead.

He loops in lazy figures half the night
Among the trees that face the corner light.

But when he brushes up against a screen,
We are afraid of what our eyes have seen.

For something is amiss or out of place
When mice with wings can wear a human face.

THEODORE ROETHKE

Cock

How many have pretended to love
This hideous, arrogant bird,
Calling quaint his vanities,
Astonishing, his energies,
And not so divinely absurd
His connections above!

They know, if the truth were known, he's not
The harbinger of dawn,
Yet perpetrate the myth that he
Resurrects the sun and daily
Crows the wonderful cycle on
That couldn't be stopped.

I detest him—that red voice
That bloodies the night with noise,
The obvious nature of his lies,
His monstrous bad taste of style and size
—And them who acclaim his joys
As if by choice.

ANTHONY OSTROFF

Trap

White, flipping
butterfly,
paperweight,

flutters by and
over shrubs,
meets a binary

mate and they
spin, two orbits
of an

invisible center;
rise
over the roof

and caught on
currents
rise higher

than trees and
higher and up
out of sight,

swifter in
ascent than they
can fly or fall.

A. R. AMMONS

The Old Falcon

She will not hunt again
In the burnished day.
Loose from her foot the chain.
She will not seek the wood
Or the Summer field.
Lift from her head the hood.

She is done with the cruel and bold,
She is done with rapacious questing.
With the light and luminous air
And the terror of beak and claw.
She will ride your wrist like a dove—
Who once had dared the breasting
Of hurricanes in the upper sky
And the threat of the lion's paw.

Now the owl will sleep on the bough
And life stir the grass in the meadow.
There will be no sound of her bells
Where the wild birds flutter and sing.
For between the earth and the sun
Has departed an evil shadow
Of death that circles with savage eyes
And drops from a pointed wing.

So let her head go free
Of its tufted hood.
She will not rise to flee
This hunter. Loose the jess.
Her implacable foot
Withers to quietness.

ELEANOR BALDWIN

Barn Swallow

A swallow skims low over the field,
Turning and darting as insects rise.
I see the blue back, orange breast, forked tail,
Pursue the motions, the bank, the dive,
The swerve in flight, a snatch at swerving flies.
He sees me also, bends his course
To skirt my presence, flutters, cries.

I like that fluttering; I only guess
At what he likes, beyond his prey.
I do not take the invisible world on trust;
Probabilities remain, and this is probable:
The flight of his outwardness, the stance of mine,
Harbor like visitants, some angel I,
Banking in timelessness, intrinsic, free.

CHARLES G. BELL

Seven Themes from the Zoo, No. 2

Like missionary priests from some bland creed,
the sacerdotal penguins veer and stomp
on wet rocks altar-wise into a spray
from rusty pipes that emphasize their pomp:
erect and fat and feathered all the way,
they lean whenever gravity shows need,
yet somehow they maintain a level sway.

In quick reversal, then, they turn and dive
into the mimic, clear, Antarctic sea
held up around the rocks by crystal glass
which, locked in space, lets doubtful humans see
that birds (or eerie more-than-birds) can pass
from sphere to deeper sphere; that they can flee
beyond dead levels of expectancy,
beyond the stupid anarchy of fact.

The penguins swim batlike through undersea.
Outside the zoo, in flowing wider lives,
the loon or grebe or water ouzel dives
through parallels to penguins joyously.

JOHN BENNETT

Visit to a Museum

In great museums one learns simple things—
That shells are colored like a sunset sky,
That birds have flame and azure on their wings,
That men and monkeys both have brains that die;
That mice have learned what even a man might learn,
How by slow effort and defeat and pain
To shun in the long labyrinth that wrong turn
Which makes the journey purposeless and vain.
But most of all I noted with amaze
The pack-rat-he of careful luminous eye,
His manners exquisite, his footstep sly,
Stealing a thread, a match, a bit of glaze,
A nail, a penny—anything that his haze
Of rattish hope thought it could profit by.

ARTHUR DAVISON FICKE

Hawk Remembered

The kestrel wakes now to the morning air,
Unhooking beak from back; casually shakes
The dust of sleep from feathers, here and there
Preening a hackle where the smoothness breaks.

And now he takes the spaces with the hymn
Of planing ease that hides the iron line
Of hungers and resolve, hanging his grim
Quest on the silk air like a flower design.

Here a land's length away within the mind
The sight reflects as memory, that still
As more important truth sails the light wind
Above the mouse life in the velvet hill

Where when reflection clicks back into sight
The recognition's swift acclaim will bring
A kind of insight into preying flight
Asleep in arm thews that once flexed a wing.

J. PHOENICE

The Stricken Colts

We pursued but to capture and destroy
The locoed colts. During the chasing hours, they turned
Their heat sprung eyes upon us.
    Their bones
All but cut through their hides.
    Hollows caverned above
The sockets of their sight and again
Where haunch and belly met. Panicked, they led
The way from range to timberline,
And there we lost the dull-coated, sweated things
Whose gait clattered over rock,
Whose breath gurgled in the throat.
    If they died there
In the mountains, it was with their soft lips,
Their young lips, thrust in snow-cold waters.

LOUISE D. PECK

Look Now, the Hawk

Look now, the hawk harries the blue heron,
angel of death from efficient heaven
whose pride of place towers above the lure.
They keep their roles according to the law.
Over the heedless water makes his pounce,
the fell falcon, and for a moment pins
and trusses her dead wing and grips her neck.
Oh, the waters break in the pebble's knock:
she cries like rust in an old wagon wheel,
he snaps her brideshead with his iron will.
The large and little feathers whirl about
in pools and ponds. Now, as I wait a bit
in lovely quiet where the river runs,
the minnows dart under shallow ruins.

MICHAEL PARR

Swan Curse

Pity you Phelim Quinn of the bogs and the fidgety finger
That burned a thunderous hole in the sagging web of the dark.
Years rust on your gun, but the sound of death shall linger
Till the heavier clap of doom. Swifter than prayer the spark
Of evil that pierced the soggy stillness and breast of a swan.
How oft the wanton pair of us saw the pale bird fetching
A shadowy meaning from sedge and shallow to press upon
The moon for an instant of awe and silence, or stretching
An arrowy neck to the salt winds jostling over the marsh.
Pity you twice, O bard of the maimed and muted tongue;
The echo of hate in the glen of the mist is hollow and harsh.
Once sang you of Children of Lir bewitched by envy to young
White swans, whose pinions were caught in the ice crest of
    the Moyle,
Aye, bound as the wings of your song are bound this wintry
    weather;
And parched is your soul tonight, as the angry scar on the soil
Where fell God's grace from the broken sky, with a bloody
    feather.

A. W. SULLIVAN

Gull

Scrapper, you don't refuse
Stern trash or galley's
Rank excess. Blessedly
Corporal, you've got carte
Blanche on the whole menu,
Give no orders,
Are never disappointed.
Plucky pragmatist, nothing
Tricks your attention.
When you sight
Down the kite string
Of your suspension, and
Dive, muck—
raker, into the wake
Of a captain's ban-
quet, you get
What you aimed for, rise
From the slow swells
Nourished, undeceived,
Resume your artful poise
Deceptively nonchalant
Above the plodding hulks
And pick your truck.

DABNEY STUART

The Rock Pool

My life could have ended then, crouched over the pool,
Wedged against Huntcliff. Absorbed in its own life,
Its pimpled sea-fronds and the slimy rocks
Spangled with barnacles, the pool lay
Deceptively clear to the sky, its wraiths of weed,
Its floating upturned dead snails, the limpets
Solidly bossed to the rock—I tried to prise them
Into a free float, but cut my fingers
And winced. Deep in the clefts stiff with mussels
I pried, and under the weed that carpeted
The pool bottom recoiled from a starfish, waylaid
A crab—there he glared, squeezed little face
Tucked under his shell. And never noticed till
A wave sploshed into my pool, stirring up sludge,
Swathing crab, starfish, limpets too, in fog,
That the tide had come up, to my ears soundlessly,
Warning me off to my world, away from the sea.

PHILIP HOBSBAUM

Genealogy of a Mermaid

She rises from coiled song of shells
Their labyrinthine wells,
Out of nuance and hue
That rocks in green and blue.

Her forms are memories of pain
Tides have swallowed; evolved again
In the snail's sad eyes
That grope for a disguise.

MORRIS WEISENTHAL

CALL HOME
THE CHILDREN

Taking Steps at Thirteen Months

she prepares to walk
with all the ritual
of a small Japanese wrestler

short stuff
with barber red and white stretched tight
over limb and torso
her head
set more so like an egg
than a real head

the sun flashing on my hot Phi Beta key
won't get in her eyes
and make her fall;
her father, B.S. degree, like a god of Greece,
sworn Officer of the Peace,
licensed to tote a gun and wear a star,
all that
won't get in her way today

she stands
Japanese-shaped
a red grain of rice
ready to begin
and the wound on her chin still burns

one foot learns something
drags the other
repeats
cheats

HEATHER ROSS MILLER

The Voyage of Jimmy Poo

A soapship went a-rocking
Upon a bathtub sea.
The sailor crouched a-smiling
Upon a dimpled knee.

Young Neptune dashed the waters
Against enamel shore,
And kept the air a-tumbling
With bubble-clouds galore.

But soon the voyage ended.
The ship was swept away
By a hand that seemed to whisper
"There'll be no more games today."

The ship lay dry and stranded
On a shiny metal tray,
And a voice was giving orders
That a sailor must obey.

Oh captain, little captain,
Make room for just one more
The next time you go sailing
Beyond enamel shore.

JAMES A. EMANUEL

After School: Room Three

One pale goldfish patrols the globe on Teacher's desk
goggles the charmed room, the blackboard's calm
assertion—the x2's. A book on the chalktray
hitches itself up like a puppy with one leg
out of its basket; a tennis shoe seeks its
tongue—a culprit—from the closet; overhead
the watercolors of Halloween wait for Thanksgiving.

A window blind blinks at "Now is the time for all
good men," and a greater truth flourishes on the wall:
"The quick brown fox." The pale goldfish learns it
all by rote; his intermittent eye pans gigantic
lessons all day long, then the night's
curriculum: blackboard, streetlight, stars.

WILLIAM STAFFORD

The El-Painter's Daughter

An empty train, grumbling through noon,
made the council of pigeons, gurgling her crumbs,
melt to a wing.

Then she walked to the place
where the El-Painter, matted with orange,
lurching in sleep, gargoyled the base
of a brooding girder.

She watched.
He shook on his back, a drowning dreamer.
Paint spooled down like toxic honey,
brocading the quivering palm of her father.
She sucked the receding dug of her ices
and turned from the shimmering dustlets of paint,
as he woke.

MILTON KESSLER

This Young Girl

This young girl, whose secret life
Vagues her eyes to the reflective, lucent
Look of the sky topping a distant
Down beyond which, invisible, lies the sea—

What does she mark, to remember, of the close things
That pearl-calm gaze now shines upon?
Her mother, opening a parasol,
Drifts over the hailed-with-daisies lawn:

Head full of designs, her father
Is pinned to a drawing board: two brothers settle
For cool jazz in the barn: a little
Sister decides to become Queen Pocahontas.

Or is it the skyline viewed from her attic window
Intimating the sea, the sea
Which far-off waits? or the water garden
Fluent with leaves and rivulets near by,

That will be her memory's leitmotif?
All seems acceptable—an old house sweetened
By wood-ash, a whole family seasoned
In dear pursuits and country gentleness.

But her eyes elude, this summer's day. Far, far
Ahead or deep within they peer
Beyond those customary things
Toward a Golden Age, which is now, is here.

C. DAY LEWIS

Burial
For Meg.

I sat on my haunches while she lined the grave
With maple leaves, patting each in place
Until no earth showed thru the dark green nest.
Then turning, she waited for me, still on her knees,
Not sure of the proper procedure next; but when
I lifted the faded grackle by the tail,
She scolded me for swinging it head down
And took her time to stroke its feathers smooth.
Stone marker set and marigolds, all done
That had to be done, she hurried across the lawn,
Withholding a suddenness of grief, to cry
Alone in her room; at twelve had learned as much
As I have learned, and neither will know more.

RICHARD C. RAYMOND

Sick Boy

Illness falls like a cloud upon
    My little frisking son:
He lies like a plant under a blight
    Dulling the bright leaf-skin.
Our culture falls away, the play
    That apes, and grows, a man
Falters, and like the wounded or
    Sick animal, his kin,
He curls to shelter the flame of life
    And lies close in his den.

Children in patient suffering
    Are sadder to see than men
Because more humble and more bewildered:
    What words can there explain
Why all pleasures have lost their savor,
    Or promise health again?
Kindness speaks from a far mountain—
    Cannot touch their pain.

ANNE RIDLER

The Gardeners

So is the child slow stooping beside him
picking radishes from the soil.
He straightens up,
his arms full of the green leaves.
She bends low to each bunch and whispers,
Please come out big and red.
Tugs at them gently to give them time to change,
if they are moody and small.
Her arms filled, she paces beside
her grandfather's elderly, puppet walk.

DAVID IGNATOW

The Stone Frog

The great stone frog doorstop
watched my passing legs
with sinister eyes. The hop
that never came dared
me to pass; I was twelve
before I knew it never cared.

GLENN PRITCHARD

A Girl Skipping Rope in Flushing

The shadow of the girl with the white
Ribbon in her hair leaps east
As she scoops the evening with her rope
And dances in dust swarming like fireflies

Over joy's cars huddling at the curb.
An airplane swims overhead, low,
Leaving bumpy, corrugated sound.
She does not hear: she concentrates on shadow

Thinning into eastern infinity.
It is a game: she leaps to escape
The other self rising on the asphalt
As the sun drops behind the cannery.

She scoops and leaps and fails.
Night rises like a lake until Flushing
Is full to its chimneys, extinguishing
Both shadow and light in her hair.

She leans on the stoop and breathes loudly.
She sees the whirling fireflies
As sun-lit dust, and her eyes burn.
Behind her eyes the rope is still alive.

STEPHEN STEPANCHEV

Daedalus to Icarus

I keep kings secret, monstrous underground,
Their peoples vacant playing with my toys:
I kill their time, bored in a boring land
While all that's upward beats behind my eyes.
My son, shall I give you wings? I gave you pride,
Part of mine born again, to play your part—
Not as these fools play, dead to worlds outside
But like your father's son, break the world's heart.
Out there you flow the round of a brimless cup
In secret, searching till the secret's won:
This is your body which I give you up,
I am your father: get me back my sun.

LOUIS COXE

Broken Shell

My smallest and last child smashed the shell
That had been given me when I was a child:
So long, so carefully kept: a pearl shell
That filled my adult hand, its immaculate
Inner dome flushed with miniature rainbow:
A tiny cave carved in far-off seas
Whose dazzle of sun-struck gold-green
Here incredibly fixed; and the sound of seas
Which was, I grew to learn, my pulse's sound.
Now dropped and broken by that child of mine
Too young to know what he has destroyed;
Too young to tell me what I should have known.

WINFIELD TOWNLEY SCOTT

The Wise Child

I couldn't wait. My childhood angered me.
It was a sickness time would cure in time,
But clocks were doctors slow to make me well.
I sulked and raged. My parents told me "play"—
I stood in the garden shouting my own name.
The noise enlarged me. I can hear it still.

At last I've come where then I longed to go.
And what's the change?—I find that I can choose
To wish for where I started. Childhood puts
Its prettiest manners on. I see the dew
Filming the lawn I stamped.
                    The wise child knows
Not here, not there, the perfect somewhere waits.

EDWARD LUCIE-SMITH

Children at Night

They dream of hoop-snakes in the darkened house,
Of water-music from half-empty jars,
And round streaked stones, of colored pasteboard cows,
The Ark, the painted trees, and shooting stars.
Awakened in the dark, they learn the sound
Of insects beating on the screen, the roll
Of military rain on roof, and ground.
They hear the ropes against the bright flagpole.
The bureau creaks; the frightened children call
The parents from a barren sleep (they bring
A glass, and light the light); along the wall
Pale crossing shadows start to dance and sing.
The interrupted dream is told, the pain
Is lost to the slow music of the rain.

SAMUEL FRENCH MORSE

PART III

OF THAT TIME,
OF THAT PLACE

At the Seed and Feed

Carrying his mandolin in the curve of afternoon
Past the hot and shaded porch
Past flead dogs and the kings of bottletop checkers
Shooting their crowed eyes beyond their strawbrimmed hats
I followed my father into the dark of an old store.

Among men and tin and bottle goods
Among bonneted ladies with crochet hoops
White tambourines etched with blue flowers
We stood in Jesus-sweet gloom.

Now Father's wizard mandolin sings the store alive
The strings lightly throbbing,
Tinkling on and on, the frets marking his fleshy fingers
His notes like plums in the dark.

Soon a fox yelps down the evening
And cows loll home spearing from a covert of trees;
Now the piney church turns yellow for Wednesday prayers
And Father, slipping the pick under the mandolin strings, bows

Dwindling in the sun.

J. EDGAR SIMMONS

The Medici Tombs

(*Michelangelo*)

She lies congealed in carven stone,
Figure of night, and endlessly
Her thoughts are known to her alone.
She sleeps, dreaming timelessly.

Dreaming, she seems all weariness
But is despair implicit here?
And does she see one star to bless
A vague darkness tinged with fear?

Companion to the stronger Day
Who is aroused intent and fierce,
And whose expression means to say
There is no dark he cannot pierce.

A soul in armor sits above
Brooding upon the sullen strife,
The intermingled hatred love
Complexities of human life.

The other's eyes are leveled, fixed.
Above the Day, above the Night.
Above the Evening and the Dawn
He gazes into endless light.

W. W. E. ROSS

Black and White Spring

There's an Italy of Titian-colours here,
And Piero backgrounds. I have seen them.
But today one long street, black with figures,
Under snow seems Breughel-white; and from
The snow-glare on the sepia-striped hills
The raw North glints up, icy, pinched and clear.
Over this hill-town migraine clouds bring chills
Of winter, stunning, shutting Spring. So nothing stirs.

And I move shrugged and taut against the spiked winds,
Ill-equipped to cope with their swift stabbing thrust
At bared street corners, craving warmth (of flesh and fire),
Release from this jawed cold that grips me—alien, lost
Among shut shuttered houses, under aching skies.
Maliciously this chilblained world deprives and binds
No Breughel-comfort; frost-black stabbing at my eyes,
Nights harsh with absence and the day's blind stare.

CHRISTOPHER HAMPTON

Turkish Garden

Perhaps it was never the flowers
Round the wind-ripe kiosk
Startled that garden to life—
Rusty doors, showers
Of cypress, crescent and griffe
Of a left-over mosque—

Perhaps the shadows thrown
On tangled reeds,
The fountain's cracked trough,
The tortured Arab script on tombstone
Taut over rough
Cool weeds.

Perhaps the garden would go back to the dead
If that script was once read.

C. A. TRYPANIS

The Cannery

In summer this town is full of rebels
Come up from Tennessee to shell the peas.

And wetbacks roam the supermarts, making
A Tijuana of the drab main street.

The Swedes and Poles who work at Wurlitzer,
And can't stand music, are all dug in:

Doors are bolted, their pretty children warned,
Where they wait for the autumnal peace.

At night the cannery's like a train,
A runaway, cans flung up like clinkers.

Sometimes on an evening hot as Southland
When even fear won't keep the windows down,

One hears the drawl of Tennessee, the quick
Laugh of Mexico in the empty streets.

LUCIEN STRYK

Chartres Cathedral

(Spengler: Decline of the West)

All souls enact an image of their dream.
The Magian and the Faustian built high.
One made an inner-space, a vault of sky,
With half-light hidden in deflected stream.
And one, with bodiless translucent gleam
That scorns material walls and passes by
All limitations and all termini,
Finds the transcendent, never the supreme.
Behold, all line dissolved in melody
And polychrome in the luciferous glass.
Form functions here, but never bodily,
And in the Gothic twilight brings to pass,
Commingled in the loftiest beam and truss,
Dark hints, vague rumors of the calculus.

DONALD C. BABCOCK

The First Day

On the Attic coast,
in Sunion,
under the Temple of Poseidon,
we swam.
Above, on the hill,
that miracle,
a boxed question,
neat, put to the god,
asking safety for
Athenian ships
sailing to the far reach
through sun-blaze
on the Aegean.
Some pillars have fallen,
but the Temple stands,
roofless, a proof
of contained space
held in pillars of wish
so simply, so level
on the hill, as to be
almost coy—
yet quietly defiant of time,
boasting the name of Byron
on a pillar, hacked (they say)
by the lover of Greece
himself, I stood in the
Temple's center,
stared down at the sea,
let the wind raise the hair
on my bare arms,
felt the god move in the air,
my first day in Greece.

NEIL WEISS

Temple Fever: Sounion

First the yellow sea-road and the sun's
steep fall where coupling shores
speak a woman of waters
adoring, adorned with islands.

                       Ascent,

the mounting of sensuous maps
upcurved to pause; land's end
and Sounion's white promise;
pillars for Poseidon.

Walk there, move through light
so startling it becomes a travel
in the shafted cores of crystal. . . .

Dissolved in shining,
ghosts for the spiral wind,
temple-seekers climb as one
to claim the jeweled distances—
and near, a marble presence,
the god locked in his stone.

JOANNE DE LONGCHAMPS

Rue St. Honore

The small baker carried bread;
He was as humble as rain.
The work of some seems a piety
Not given to us all to share
In quite the same way.

But in this way or that
There is an excellence for all to find,
Each in his own fashion,
Not measured by the Slave of Michelangelo
Or Chartres, built firm and clear
Over the Druids' well,
But grown from anyone
In a small way daily.
You can find it
In the smell of coffee, freshly made,
Or of the baker's oven
Where in the evening's dull warmth
The cricket cries
Improvident:
We feel his small cry
Is ours.
His ceaseless song
With our small light
Defeats the darkness
Of the grave.

PETER WILLIAMSON

Looking at the Empire State Building

It is still the Tallest Building in the World.
(Although they are already busy changing that)
Coming as I do from the Great Plains,
it has been my Holy Mountain from the beginning.
When it disappears past clouds, I imagine
the gods holding a picnic—for once
happily masked from our stares.
At night when the top is lighted
I see it as my Holy Volcano
and the biggest penny-bank anywhere.
It is the only present I would ever
have liked to give Jean Harlow.
Planes and birds are known to crash into it.
I can't help expecting any minute
to see poor King Kong fall from the dirigible mast
or spot lovely Melisande leaning out from an upper floor
to let down her long golden hair.

RALPH POMEROY

Sea News

Wanderer without home, my memory goes,
By a steep path, along a sea-bent shore,
Where high-pitched gulls are vending our old news,
The fortunes of our lost and lovely war

Made in a blown-away remembered house
Drenched through with salt to make a nameless tree,
(In every storm our garden was the beach
So cheek by jowl we neighbored with the sea)

And closer to each other that wild dark
When fear was a cold lodger in our bones,
Praying the wrenching roof away from flight,
The walls to hold against the thrashing stones.

What cracks the heart is never in the storm.
Bright as the day that followed you were there,
And went away in such a gathered calm
The gulls were poised like vultures on the air.

Wanderer without home, my memory goes,
By a steep path, along an empty beach,
Where high-pitched gulls are vending our old news,
And sea is loneliness beyond my reach.

ERIC BARKER

Tamazunchali

The corn comes flowing down the hills
Like water with tall crests the while,
And every color there is fills
Each rounded top and each defile.

· 244 ·

Clouds crowd over the road you pass
And naked children leap from them
To show you bits of rocky glass
As though these were a diadem.

WITTER BYNNER

Above the Nile

In his cliff-carved tomb
At Aswan sits the pharaoh,
Hands on knees, long eyes
Set beyond sandstone lintel
To dim-lit levels of the Nile;

Over the fronting ledges
The sun sends one beam pointing
To his eyes, then down the trunk,
Settling finally at his feet.

They've moved the tomb now
High above the flooded Nile,
But that shaft of day flies
From a Numidian sky of light
Eyes still sightless after
Such a miracle.

HORACE E. HAMILTON

Egypt

Descending towards Cairo, an arid
plain is like a misted mirror, its haze
the diffused image of the sun. Egypt
is straw to the sun's flame, its monuments
are slipping into the floodwaters like beasts
come to drink from the dry interior.

Cranes stand like herons in pools of concrete
where slaves once tore their muscles so that kings
might lie entombed in cool, musk-smelling darkness,
mummified, perfect as butterfly specimens:
the more advanced a civilization,
the subtler the refinement of vanity.

The same old Egypt holds its sun-wearied earth
together with transfusions from the Nile,
the dammed-up waters a bank of the country's blood.
The concrete lifts its pharaoh head above
the people in Cairo, compelling submission
to the hours of work. The sky is a scrap of iron.

A scholar hurries to a museum,
a tourist points his zoom lens at flies
sticking to a cluster of dates in a bazaar.
Second-hand vision records Egypt, myths
endure. The same old Egypt contracts like
a dried fig in the heat of the jet's ascent.

ZULFIKAR GHOSE

Night in November

From Leo rain the Leonids;
The coastal towns are clear tonight.
Andromeda's anfractuous lids
Burn with a spectral anthracite.

In from the sea the splendid ships
Find continent a rising shelf;
The whistler, red with moistened lips,
Is festival unto himself.

Grief and the grave are empty words:
The vast inchoate claims the soul
As surely as dawn's shoreward birds
Will find the sky an empty bowl.

DAVID MCCORD

Oxford

I remember when I saw for the first time,
Beyond the factory yards and chimneys,
The celebrated undulating line
Of massive walls and domes and spires.
The sun just down behind it all,
It seemed that evening
Like a black exotic dragon of the deep,
Surfaced in the distance on the sea,
Its habitat the timeless and unknown.
Now to this day I do not quite accept
That there are those who speak of it
Familiarly, though I in turn
Was to be bored there,
And was to love it only as I would.

RICHARD ALDRIDGE

Himalaya

In the garden of my soul
Please walk tenderly
The grass on the lawn
Is only newborn
Do not pluck the lotus
Let it come into bloom
Let it fade within itself
As a wish is perfected

The unfrozen stream
From Himalayas
Warms the kicking feet
Of the children sitting
Near the creek
The gauzy fog still
Lingers around the peak

A chant, then an echo, an echo
As century follows century
Starlight, moonlight and sun
The explained and unexplained
Symbols of Heaven

My soul has traveled far and far
And thinks no otherwise
Here, here is my paradise.

PO FEI HUANG

Emigrant's Iconoclasm

As if a left-handed god had placed my village
so dangerously on that slope where even dogs
sheltered their heads under rocks when barking.

Sheltered cocks crowed always at sunset. Grapes
taught a serious winter drunkenness. At spring
not the young but the old died all the same.

Not the sea but the mountains waved
over my village while it shook like a ship
now at the bottom of the valley, then up above it.

Now sheltering under dogs, the shepherds
walk on rocks scattered by giants, two months
after their King's wedding. Like confetti.

After escaping from my village, I found a city
where a god's right hand signals the traffic
and I step over the bodies of bored, rightless men.

TANER BAYBARS

The Autostrada

Like all great thoughts that revolutionize
The world, it runs direct and broad and simple,
And so much obvious that for centuries
On end nobody thought it. Rip and rimple,
It shares the lightning's nature and the light's
In non-regardance of impediment.

What Alps it tunnels, what abysms it bridges,
And what parochial feuds it cuts clean through,
Scorning the flood's and avalanche's edges,
Men speeding hardly now remember. Night's
Arrivals, dawn's departures to their view
Blend all as one, in one supreme event
About to be. For they have long accepted
This road that outraged once their settled habit
As common highroad of their daily thinking;
Its gold end answers back their far desire,
Their endless vehicles that flash along it
Spark from its current's universal fire.

GEOFFREY JOHNSON

Capturing a Spring

Near Seven Springs, where the Churn rises, is Calmsden,
Straggling illogically along the Chedworth road;
There's not much of it, a few brick houses, modern
And raw, and round a bend in the road some old
Ones of Cotswold stone, weathered and mellow,
Seeming to grow out of the bank where they stand in a row.

Then, when there seems to be no more, from under
A Celtic cross, rooted in a mound, tumbles the spring,
Showering its gift upon parched travellers,
Lone source of sweet water, offering drink,
Drawing us to feel its coolness and dabble
In the pool beneath, then lie in the shade by its babble.

A farmer, who has just fed his pigs in the opposite
Field, puts away his pails and crosses the road
To drink, and soon a shepherd with a black and white
Collie joins him to capture the bubbling flow
In a lemonade bottle, while the dog puts his front paws
On the rim of the pool, his head between, and laps.

When I hear the allegro rhythms of a city fountain
I shall think of this spring I did not wish to leave,
Water in a dry season, bounding out of limestone;
I shall sit in the concrete square and almost believe
I can hear the singing of secretive stones in the hills,
Where rain water gathers beneath dark earth and spills.

ROSEMARY JOSEPH

Rocks Partly Held in Mist

The rocks out in this bay
are partly held in mist.
Their ragged top is seen
but at their base a froth-
like substance hangs as if
the element of ice from which
shroud-like vapors rise
clung fiercely to each cliff.

And so with other things
whose upper parts shine in
the light that they have reached,
whose lower half is held
as if by a terrible past
by all the weight and darkness,
characteristics of the earth.

The force that hangs around
the base of rocks needs ghosts
and other shapes to fall
like mist across the mind,
to gather strength in bones,
in lack of clarity, in fear.
Slowly the top and upper parts
dissolve in air as air.

ARTHUR GREGOR

Imperial Valley, Calif.

From snows packed on barren mountains
these cold blue waters run
down canyons through wastes to fountains
where fruit trees take the sun;

there farmers have from God's nothing,
from parched air and dry loam,
made water amount to something
and given life a home.

Yet civil farmers breed wild sons,
and in night's cold blue sky
their barbarous imaginations
dream where new deserts lie

bare for settling: those silver lands
where cunning men will go
to build Karnak on moon-bleak sands
that civil fruits may grow.

JASCHA KESSLER

The Ramblers

Nobody knows who planted those pink roses
Down along the railroad track, nor how long
Ago (except that it was at least three wars back)
They ramble down the bank beside the rails
Like a crowd of teenage girls, who, leaving
Sunday School to go home by the woods,
Have mussed up their best dresses, roaming so.

The roses have tenacity. Their pink endures.
They were, I suppose, in a dooryard garden
When there were trees along that then country
Street, and a coal-stove in the kitchen,
And Wednesday was the night for Missionary Meeting.
Pink Roses. One whole generation leaps
To life, all of a piece, flickering wanly

In my mind, like an old-time movie, when I
Ride the train. Click and clack along the track
It goes. I see the roses and remember
The grape-arbor out back, homemade lemonade,
And old folks on the front porch, sitting straight
In creaking wicker chairs—talk, talk, talking
About Lincoln—damning John Wilkes Booth.

VIRGINIA LINTON

The Sea House

Nobody knows what is in the black house
By the sea or why it should be closed to the light.
No doubt its rooms are rounded with sticky webs,
Its entryways cushioned by veridian moss. Perhaps
A Franklin stove beside a monumental bed
Is still inside. Only clouds full of rain,
Dark above the water, enter this property.
Gusts of wind fill the lot with masses
Of blue fog and fairly inaudible thunder.
It is no wonder tenants have boarded up the door.
The house hugs the shore; its slant of roof
And chimney width seem bolted to the earth.
Its shingles curl like petals or dry leaves.

This house is better than a stone set up
To mark a grief. It resembles a lantern,
Shining through a window in the early afternoon,
Put down to signal some disaster that
Bare voices have no strength to say . . . that the fog
Has sealed up in an unmarked ledge and wave.

WILLIAM GOODREAU

Near Mons

Swallowing snow
out of the shell pits,
where the soldier's bones
rot like ribs
of ancient leaves,
the spring washes
these northern fields
like nuggets
smeared with light.

Set up the watchmen
so we can all wake up
after bombardment
lifting the mud
out of our boots.
No one is allowed
to start over again,
not even God.

In the soft fields
the leaves turn green;
the same birds
nest in the ricks;
now and then
farmers turn up
an unused shell,
while dropping the seeds
in the soft cracks
like upturned fists.

NEIL MYERS

Morning at the Temple of Kobai

In the cold room
the other side of the cardboard wall
at five-thirty in the morning
the priest sounds his drum and bells,
chants, coughs, chants.

From under the electric blanket
the undecipherable sutra
of the complete law
only a paper-thickness away
stirs, reassures, lulls.

Birds of dawn are noisy in the garden
invisible past the white paper
pasted on wooden lattices,
but they and the man up in the early morning
fade from the mind in the bed's warmth.

Every morning I am awakened
but before the priest is quiet
fall back to sleep again
meaning to ponder birds and Buddha
but returned to the phantom world of dreamed emotions.

When I reawake to reality
I slide back all the paper walls,
let warmed daylight into the room,
and say good morning to the priest
now out sweeping a night's fallen leaves from the moss.

EDITH SHIFFERT

In Cycle Repeated
(*Mérida—Spain*)

Before fruit, the flower
Before bud, the seed.
Passion and need
Mark earth's measure.
Conquering men
Sandaled or booted,
Bled and were rooted
Deep in their grain.
Cork-oak and olive,
Roof-tree and hearth,
Alien earth
Stubborn to give,
Yielded a richer
Harvest, and fed
Living and dead,
A turbulent mixture
Of breakers and builders.
They dreamt a town
Spaciously grown
With Roman vistas,
Arched, columned and watered.
It rose on the plain.
Now broken again
In cycle repeated.

KATHERINE GARRISON CHAPIN

The River

Green silk, or a shot silk, blue
Verging to green at the edges,
The river reflects the sky
Alas. I wish that its hue
Were the constant green of its sedges
Or the reeds it is floating by.

It reflects the entrances, dangers,
Exploits, vivid reversals
Of weather over the days,
But it learns to make these changes
By too many long rehearsals
Of overcasts and grays.

So let it take its station
Less mutably. Put it to school
Not to the sky but the land.
This endless transformation,
Because it is beautiful,
Let some of it somehow stand.

But seeing the long streak quiver
There in the distance, my eye
Is astonished and unbelieving.
It exclaims to itself forever:
This water is passing by!
It arrives and yet it is leaving!

DONALD DAVIE

The Wall

Sunlight doesn't go on making
And making its reappearances on that stained wall
Without alteration. It's getting
More elderly, I would say; goes a mellower course
Over chair-dent and sweat-mark,
Moving a window-square which seems
Not so clear now at the edges. To have
Sat once among such motes and specks
Was to be glad to see dust made quick
By illumination, interruption by liveness.
This dust now is literal dust, shown up
By this changed also sun as wandering in air
As thinking wanders in the aged—with
An unkind pleasantness. Such sun
Used not to calm me near to sleep like this.

ALAN BROWNJOHN

THINGS . . .
AND OTHER THINGS

They Make a Lovely Pretense

They make a lovely pretense swaying there
Or bobbing gently under the dark earlobes
As if, attached, they gave themselves to air
And made of light small lanterns, turquoise globes.
They seem to give their colors everywhere
To daily things that brighten in their flowing,
The gentled cheek, the neckline and the hair,
As if their motion touched us into glowing.
But once removed, they show an imperfection
And surface pales a little in its shade.
Without the radiance of some reflection
The naked eye might freeze or see them flawed
As imitation, and we ourselves become
Worthless as gemstone, leaving our light hands numb.

PHILIP LEGLER

Lines Based on a 1924 Advertisement

Moon Cars, that race of ghosts, but once "the world's
Fastest expanding maker of motor cars"—
Where are the "different" people in their Moon cars,
Sly-grogging on cold Prohibitionist nights
In leather seats scudding down asphalt highways,
The blasé Moon riders mad as mineral water,
Chucking champagne glasses in camellia bushes?
Wild as the beautiful eyes of Zelda Fitzgerald,
Delicate as nasturtiums, Moon drivers crash
Down gorges, overturn in deserts, tumble off headlands.
Telephones ring in their darkened bungalows,
Oysters and avocadoes rot in the ice-box,
But they have vanished into the ultraviolet,
Sleepy with carbon monoxide and leaving no message.

GEOFFREY LEHMANN

Objet d'Art

The copper bowl I keep
    Tobacco
In is thick with nightingales

And roses, up to the
    Minaret
Its lid, incised so-so.

I no longer smoke in
    Company,
It seems indecent:

Reminded by those birds
      And flowers
Of a botched renown,

A Persian I once
      Had for tea
Turned from it and wept.

LUCIEN STRYK

Honey

This tilted jar
Urges amber flow;
Ambrosial
Material,
Thick stuff, loath
And slow
To yield its sloth
And grudgingly transmute
Its liquid attribute.
Two elements at war;
Glacier in miniature.

MELVILLE CANE

The Vial

Reflecting all,
Dazzling, symmetrical,
Devoid of trait,
Little of which I could not hold
The distillate,

Whatever shade,
Gamut of retrograde
Viscosity,
But emptied of all save manifold
Transparency,

Misuse or dust
Inhibiting my trust,
Become opaque,
Contaminative to all, weird-scrolled,
Deemed fit to break.

Whether my own
Or merely those once shown,
I seep a strength,
And shall, of unknown powers the mold,
Blast joy at length.

DAVID GALLER

Salt

Salt for white
And salt for pure.
What's salted right
Will keep and cure.

Salt for cheap
And salt for free.
The poor may reap
Salt from the sea.

Salt for taste
And salt for wit.
Be wise. Don't waste
A pinch of it.

ROBERT FRANCIS

Kite

Neither lighter nor heavier
For having known a white while of air,
Still I retie my heart to the tail
Of a weathering kite and sail
High heavier than the sky
Using the sky to move by.

I am deliberately aware
All old kites inherit
The ills of every soared kite.

But kites have always been intended
To dance sky at the farthest end
Of a human hand until night.

HOLLIS SUMMERS

Alum

This alum crystal:
a poet's double-bedded pyramid
built on one square base
        obliterates for a moment
the skidding progress of our partial
        knowledge,
our blindfold march across the desert, Time.
        We shed the human mantle,
we stand at the center of the six point cross.

For one moment we rest, unlost,
      in the crystal seeing ourselves
as would a Creator. Then on we ramble
forgetting and forgotten in unsymmetry.

RICHARD BURNS

The Willow Switch

I plucked a willow switch
That grew beside the ditch,
And felt it writhe and twist
In terror to evade
The prison of my wrist;
The short fierce struggle ripped
The red-gold bark to show
Defenseless beauty stripped:
The ivory flesh below
The silk of jade.

Now at my lightest touch
It sings and springs with such
Abandon, it must be
Happier in my hand
Than when it flourished free.
And I have found delight
Feeling my mastery,
Swinging it through the bright
And crystal air, but see—
Though hard to understand—
It has imprisoned me.

DOUGLAS GIBSON

Catalpa Trees

Catalpa tree with trunk like monolith,
Wide-reaching branches and a thick of leaves
As green as is lush grass
And wide as open hands.

And I remember how your blossoms came
Amid the freshness of your large green leaves,
Whiter than seagulls' breasts,
A thousand thousand blooms.

And like men of good heart who proffer all,
Descending branches held out boons to us,
Bunches of blossoms rare,
White, freaked and delicate.

Then strewed them on the ground, and distances
Being native to these trees, strewed them so deep
For prairie winds to sweep
Across unbounded lands.

PADRAIC COLUM

The Water Wants All Sea

The seawall goes to show you can cut water
Provided the blade stay in the slice. The green
Rind of the sea is clearly through itself
A morning melon where it meets the knife
Clean-edged and yellowing and lipped with dew

But has not the composure of the fruit:
The surface bulks and bulges, breaks and sprays
Lipping and lapping, clambering and is repulsed,
Is lifted again, claps, lapses and drifts away
And word of this goes every baffled where.

The wharfpoles in their silver-gray old age
Find second greenhood in the waterooze
Warping into the clasp and lisp of waves.
The waterhands deal gently with their sides
Framing all gestures in an act of love.

The sea slides in between to try its spite
On the presumption that looks down on it.
This water wants all sea, unwearied wishing
Will wear the world away or one dark night
Lifting its head from sleep, will leap the brim.

There where the sloping flattery of beach
Persuades it this is so, it stops, put off
By the soft answer; turns its head, content;
Then seized with doubt returns to ask once more
More searching questions; more and more of these.

Here's no equivocation and no doubt.
Here's war to the death. The ocean's half alive
And—angered by the deadness of the thing
That still affronts it, blunt, unmuscular—
Rises and ever rises to the challenge;

While we, impermanently heighted here,
Look down into the boiling mind that once
Whipping itself, storming its own walls
Battered and broke the basement gates of life
Not knowing what lay behind in its blind pride.

LLOYD FRANKENBERG

The Lie

Only a few it touched at first
Believed the lie to be accurst,
    Felt the sly rot
    Of what was not.

And even they said, "Let it go,
Never another needs to know;
    If it happens again
    We'll stop it then."

Only a drop or so of ink
Was spent in making all men think
    Their very eyes
    Saw otherwise.

This drop of ink, in seven days,
Had darkened all the seven seas—
    "Not very much,"
    Men cried, "a mere touch."

But no man's patience and devotion
Analyzed any piece of ocean,
    Which rolled on shore,
    Darker than before.

The ocean and the ink together,
The lie become part of the weather,
    Indelibly meant
    And permanent.

HOWARD NEMEROV

The Opposition

Tense with infallibility,
we argued over now what none
of us remembers. Victory
was all. Debates were to be won.

Later we passed without a word
as if the things we said were lies,
and lies the only things we heard.
We still avoid each other's eyes.

SAMUEL HAZO

Hug Your Hunger, Brother

Hug your hunger, brother.
Do not barter, brother,
Other hungers for your own.

Have you known another
Hunger that could be a brother
To your own?

Choose a hunger, brother,
To exceed your wants, other
Goading hungers of the flesh and bone.

Know your hunger, brother,
As another
Hunger of my own.

RYAH TUMARKIN GOODMAN

Precedents

Precedents
Are lumbering locomotives,
Old timers
Laboring up a long grade,
Puffing asthmatic steam
Behind a creaky row of brown freight cars,
Pushing them forward.

When was it
That we have shunted them off,
Left them on a sidetrack
To swallow their own smoke?
Who was it hitched on
Ahead of the whole outfit
A new, powerful super-engine pulling it
Jerkily out of its pace
Sending a sudden row of rusty chuckles
All the way down the line?

Freight train
So incredibly long
Its caboose, painted red,
Rolling over the rails, hammering
At the other end of the world.

ISRAEL NEWMAN

Force of Illusions

There was the butcher's hand.
He squeezed it and the blood
Spurted from between the fingers
And fell to the floor.
And then the body fell.

So afterward, at night,
The wind of Iceland and
The wind of Ceylon,
Meeting, gripped in mind,
Gripped it and grappled my thoughts.

The black wind of the sea
And the green wind
Whirled upon me.
The blood of the mind fell
To the floor. I slept.

Yet there was a man within me
Could have risen to the clouds,
Could have touched these winds,
Bent and broken them down,
Could have stood up sharply in the air.

WALLACE STEVENS

On Lighting the Fire

Quick, quick you
claw of fire,
rip up the log's law,
logic the liar;

build a ruby
den beneath,
tear down substance
with soft teeth.

I'll live within
your house of spirit,
a salamander,
when I can bear it,

or basilisk
with scarlet breath,
reduced to gem
by your quick death.

Quick translator,
robber of shape,
show how chaos
roars agape,

its ecstatic ash
the core
of color only,
raw and pure.

MAY SWENSON

No Curtain

From stone to arrow, sling-shot, gun,
Rifle and rocket, roadways run.
Hammer and sickle, old as fable,
Die with the smithy and the stable.

Creators of the live machine
We quit the lanes of what has been
Forced by the atom and the jet
To cross the gulphs our hatreds set.

         Laws are less quick
         Than wheel and rod
         To change the attributes
         Of God.

         One truth is certain:
         Iron makes no curtain.

F. R. SCOTT

Trapezists

The trapezist
the proud one
with no nets,
apotheosis
of artist,
discerning
discipline,
courts Death; flaunts it;
achieves evolutionary surety
after infinite trips; care.
And one minute,
there he is!
Poised
in purity;
perfect
balanced cross
against air!

DAISY ALDAN

In Old Age

In old age, I should like to remember this morning's
Excursion on the ornamental lake,
Among swans and flowery islets

Where we make pretense of having no problems
Deeper than the shallow craft,
The hardly thigh-deep water

The swans remind me of Schlotheim:
Its frozen, sun-filled winters,
Its rose-enamored summers.

BRENDA CHAMBERLAIN

THE TURNING SEASONS

In Autumn

The rowan routs the green eastern hills;
The quick, the chilly, wind comes gusting on;
Down falls the river as the stripped land wills;
Hot, hungry Summer shakes a carillon
Of leaves, in leaving earth and men alone.
A sting pulsates the blood; life makes a heat
Better than sullen sun to warm the bone.
The striding foot begins anew to fleet
And run, toeing lazed hours and dream behind.
Senses unleashed are lusty for good living;
Stretched muscles bound to serve the spurring mind;
The wind whips wild and sharp to fresh gale-giving;
The witty frost repaints each banished flower;
The nostril feels the flux of winy cold;
Each head lifts high; each marking eye grows bold;
The crackling, fine-spun moments heap the hour.

GENE DERWOOD

Cold August

The sun had shrunk to a dime,
passing behind the smallest
of clouds; the field was root
bare—shorthorns had grazed
it to leather. August's coldest
day when the green, unlike
its former self, returned to earth
as metal. Then from a swamp
I saw two large shadows floating
across the river, move up the sloping
bank, float swiftly as shadows against
the field toward where I stood.
I looked up as two great, red-tailed
hawks passed overhead; for an instant
I felt as prey then wheeled to watch
them disappear in southward course.
A day born in cold sourness
suffused me then in its dark,
brief image of magnificence.

JIM HARRISON

Dusk in the Sugar Woods

The sap was liquid light from spout to
     pail,
His cask stood loaded for the day's last
     run,
But now, though man might tire and
     sunlight fail,
The maples had awakened. Where the
     sun
Sent cold red lances through the thin-
     ning wood
He saw the morrow's buckets in his
     mind
And took the season's measure. Earth,
     the blind
Dark earth was singing, and the song
     was good.

He tallied his tomorrow, and his thought
Recalled a fern's thin feather where
     the noon
Had warmed a maple's roots. The light
     bit colder.
Good night, he told the wood. Be strong,
     but not
For maples: for the fern one day too
     soon
Looking for Spring upon a mountain
     shoulder.

CHARLES MALAM

Aspects

Clean in the light, with nothing to remember,
The fox fur shrivels, the bone beak drops apart;
Sludge on the ground, the dead deer drips his heart.

Clean in the weather, trees crack and lean over;
Mountain bows down and combs its scurfy head
To make a meadow and its own deathbed.

Clean in the moon, tides scrub away their islands,
Unpicking gulls. Whales that have learned to drown,
Ballooning up, meet navies circling down.

Clean in the mind, a new mind creeps to being,
Eating the old. . . . Ancestors have no place
In such clean qualities as time and space.

NORMAN MAC CAIG

Dead Metaphors

There used to be a time when, like Kate now in the lane,
I could sweep up a pile of leaves—and sweep up autumn!
She has left her token now; she has forgotten them already.
(They were not even ours to clear: they just happened to lie
    there generous)
She skirmishes and goes, leaving her metaphor's energy in the
    air

I work on, on my side, dragging them into tummocks,
Pressing crisp gold between boards, wheeling light loads away.
But I can no longer gain achievement between my teeth
Against a whole end to a world.
    They are still drifting thick from the elms:
By the time I've done, the path is recovered with yellow.

Better to lean on the broom and cherish the rare last touch
While the half-torn gilded sprays are paler than last blue sky,
And the ground is rich, with asphalt pools among beaches.
Soon all will be blackened and bare: as yet this brooming
    is folly.

But Kate kicked them up and won, with a flurry of dismissal:
It is me the leaves dismiss: in my sense of futile scratching
As at a closing door I succumb to an inward grimace
Where my gratitude for the last cold sun of November
Is mocked by apparent wealth that masks decay's savageries.

DAVID HOLBROOK

At Thanksgiving

Brown on brown stretches the pastureland,
Brown on brown, and hill becomes horizon:
A somber splendor those born to it know,
Bone and fiber, year on turning year.
Sparrow and pheasant break the silence of birds
But briefly, and the wind protests the trees;
The creeks are louder over fallen limbs,
And louder in the cold, clear air the crows
Call and quarrel over the shelterbelts
That strand the wind where it would have its way.

For this it was, not in some winter fear,
We labored out long summer half-content:
To hear the wind frustrated into song,
To find the promise kept, desire's end.
Oh if this house might follow in its season,
Might tower here amid the permanence
Of shifting fields and seasons as they turn
And root its generations in old truth:
For this the summer came, for this the spring,
The green we covet in this brown on brown.

JO ANN LEICHLITER

Benediction

Thus now, as on the face of one new-dead,
The tremendous and translucent marble peace,
The passion spent, the violent word long said;
So on this land the winter brings its own surcease.

Whatever thunders and green fevers of the summer brewed,
Whatever poisonous bright hope flowered there;
Now all is quiet within the rigid leafless wood,
Now all is silent in the cold immobile air.

Beautiful in chill austerity, the frosted bough,
Untroubled by the flight or sad-sweet song of bird;
Whatever burned another season there is ended now:
The bitter act, the transient leaf, the spoken word.

FREDERICK EBRIGHT

Rain on South-East England

This place is so much
Mauled, I have to think
Others besides these Dutch
And low green counties drink
The summer rains, before
I hold it in my mind
What a soft rain is for:
To ease, flush through, unbind.
Tightly starred, on the flat
Marred ground once, with a thin
Unambitious mat
I mended England's ruin.
Growth these last years works
My roots into the air;
Aspiring on long stalks,
My blooms digest no fare
Coarser than light. The strain
Of self-enhancement frees:
I take no care for the rain,
Soured soil, and shattered trees.

DONALD DAVIE

Seasons

Greasy snow remnants
melting in the pasture, cards
splayed from an old deck.

Hear night bellow, our
great black bull; and now the dawn
distantly lowing.

Summer's dusk of silk
is autumn's worsted and now
winter's dry linen.

Once I carried time
like a stone. Now I wear it
like mist on my sleeve.

Dawn, hoar on the grass,
deer knee-deep in crispness. Ah,
baby, snuggle down.

HAYDEN CARRUTH

Man Watching

Is it the horse explains the field,
Which he exists to crop; or that the field

Is only grown at all to make
The horse's nourishment?

                    Whichever way,
The two can yield, at dawn, an
Aesthetic incident: slight mist,

The slow grass growing, the slow
Horse turning; and the man

Watching as he stands in the first sun
On the revolving earth.

ALAN BROWNJOHN

Sap Bucket Song

We tap the sugar bush and tap a world.
No longer numbed by ice, we grow aware
of wide horizons; and the year, unfurled,
shakes out its catkins on the fragrant air.
Distinct and poignant as a single string
struck by a loving and remembering hand
in rooms no longer used, the sap of Spring
taps in the pails of sugar maple land.

Winter is gone. The sunlight visibly lingers
on the high boughs, the northward-flying birds.
We point the birds out with our thawing fingers,
and Winter leaves us in a rush of words
that gives new meaning to old verities
like the thin sweetness running from the trees.

LOUIS STODDARD

Summer Afternoon

To zig-zag with the ant
Through grass-topped jungles, sway
In many-masted trees with birds, hand fluttering
Over the tiger-lilies with the lone
White butterfly, anything, anything
But sitting here sheltered from the sun,
While all around me the summer
Burns, beats, and blazes
From sun to sky to green—
Hot, naked, unashamed beauty!

RAYMOND SOUSTER

Northbound

Leaving tropic parallels
For Northern desolation,
I like to trace declining trends
In Southern vegetation.

The palm trees are the first to go—
By Carolina, lost—
Like youthful flarings, much too frail
To stand maturing frost.

Next, the live oak; then resinous pine;
Then wild savannahs fade,
Absented by climatic rules
As stern as latitude.

Transition ends on Maine's rock hills,
Beyond thick glades and loam;
An ancient thorn tree, twisted skies
Welcome the traveler home.

LARRY RUBIN

Northern View

Day comes slowly up north,
From the first thin white of dawn's
Beginning to the last gold, dissolving
When the long beams of the sun at last
Lie level on the earth. It comes as slowly
As our trees grow, our apples ripen,
Or the day turns toward the night.
We have a long time to think about change
And to be tempered to what will come.
We have a long time to hold life
Within our hands and savor it
And know it good—juniper and oak,
From laying the fire to the last pale smoke.

HARRIET PLIMPTON

Spidersilk

A resident of Spider Hill,
He'd watched the fat arachnoid moon
Suck many a hapless afternoon
Grotesquely pale.

And watched while winter's hairy legs
Traversed the cold horizon-loom,
Tangling the bleak world in a net
Of snowy doom.

Most glamorous to him, of course,
Was that dim spider who crochets,
Without discernible remorse,
The web of days—

Who caught him, (to his unsurprise)
And dined upon his hands and face
And tied the bones up in a piece
Of loamy lace.

JOHN NIXON, JR.

In Early Spring

Now that the world of snow
And dark still hours have gone,
We put on boots and go
To see what has been done
To woods and well and lawn.

We notice sheath and bud
On each bare bush and tree,
But trudging through the mud
With all the landscape dun,
Know nonetheless that we

Will take it in surprise
When one day soon the new
Appears through such disguise—
As we have always done,
As men will always do.

RICHARD ALDRIDGE

Apology

Yes, it is true: I can remember now
coming out of work and leaving death
behind the Clinic doors, remarking how
Spring unmistakably was on the street:
as many blocks as we could see were sweet
with evening, breathing a new breath,
and in the park the crocuses were whole,
and grass was strong. Yes, Spring did waken
a residue of worship in the soul.
Yet we were quick to name it: home to love
is animal and timely in the Spring,
and we could bear the spirit's being shaken
even by resurrection, if our eyes
could turn from that warm life awakening
to hearts like motors, impersonal and wise.

But mostly days were hurried, with no time:
like city noons; as many horns to scream:
as many men: as many vehicles:
we watched the nervous stoplight for the "Go."
We could not traffic there with miracles
or question whence we came, or what sublime
appointment we should keep: we did not know—
Oh, God, forgive us that we did not know—
and that we did not even dream!

EDITH HENRICH

Between Motions

Like flies that summer, night would always break
first over the lodge roof and hover there,
declining finally to the glistering lake
below where lovers in their craft seized at the air.
And in that motion, on the topmost floor,
we watched it come, drenching the sunlight down,
as if some rower, having plied his oar,
had pulled the darkness and the lake to one
so that all moved to oneness in his reaches.
Inside that oneness like a spreading cloak,
we threshed until the sunlight's dull increases
cut softly as the plash of a second stroke
through night's dark air, revealing day's sharp beeches
and flyswarms lighting upward, slit to pieces.

JEROME MAZZARO

The First Night of Fall and Falling Rain

The common rain had come again
Slanting and colorless, pale and anonymous,
Faintly falling in the first evening
Of the first perception of the actual fall.
The long and late light had slowly gathered up
A sooty wool of clouded sky, dim and distant more and more
Until, at dusk, the very sense of selfhood waned,
A weakening nothing halted, diminished or denied or set aside,
Neither tea, nor, after an hour whiskey,
Ice and then a pleasant glow, a burning,
And the first leaping wood fire
Since a cold night in May, too long ago to be more than
Merely a cold and vivid memory.
Staring, empty and without thought
Beyond the rising mists of the emotion of causeless sadness,
How suddenly all consciousness leaped in spontaneous
    gladness;
Knowing without thinking how the falling rain (outside, all
    over)
In slow sustained consistent vibration all over outside
Tapping window, streaking roof, running down runnel and
    drain
Waking a sense, once more, of all that lived outside of us,
Beyond emotion, far beyond the swollen distorted shadows
    and lights
Of the toy town and the vanity fair of waking consciousness!

DELMORE SCHWARTZ

OCCASIONAL . . .

For a Wine Festival

Now the late fruits are in.
Now moves the leaf-starred year
Down, in the sun's decline.
Stoop. Have no fear.
Glance at the burdened tree:
Dark is the grape's wild skin.
Dance, limbs, be free.
Bring the bright clusters here
And crush them into wine.
Acorns from yellow boughs
Drop to the listening ground.
Spirits who never tire,
Dance, dance your round.
Old roots, old thoughts and dry,
Catch, as your footprints rouse
Flames where they fly,
Knowing the year has found
It's own more secret fire.
Nothing supreme shall pass.
Earth to an ember gone
Wears but the death it feigns
And still burns on.
One note more true than time
And shattered falls his glass.
Steal, steal from rhyme:
Take from the glass that shone
The vintage that remains.

VERNON WATKINS

The Cocktail Party

Who is it stands trembling
Plucking as on a violin
Each sound to make it clear?
Am I calling from within?

Is this face, so unrelaxed
With smiles of courtesy or dubious chagrin
Is this face another self
That holds me in?

I know that guest, lame and thin, has gone to war.
The other, who holds his face so taut,
Has been to China, rather far:
I only travel as I let my door ajar.

These faces taunt me now.
My masks fall.
I am the one the other
My fumbling will extends to each.

I hold the cocktail glass and shudder.
Will it shatter to the floor?
And shall I at home pick the pieces up—
My scattered will, the strangers' faces, the broken cup?

I flip my heart to the other side.
Is it I? Is it I?
I decide to hold the glass
And let the question ride.

HARRIET ZINNES

In a Warm Chicken House

Gerard de Nerval,
Locked in prison in 1832,
Under a liberal regime,
Prayed for some green thing
In the winter.
He spoke, aloud, to a bird dividing space
Into breezes and horizons.

This afternoon, in 1960, I sit, all alone,
At the end of the Eisenhower administration,
Counting the blades of gold outside the window
Of a warm chicken house, near the border
Of South Dakota.

Gerard de Nerval was still young, his eyes nested
In green moss.
He felt ivy gracefully entering his soul
Through the bars of the prison window.
I am so delighted with his season of rare plants,
I have just paused in my own poem,
To step outside and fetch one of those blades of golden grass
To mark a page in his book,
One of those precious things I had forgotten to love.

JAMES WRIGHT

A Dream of Apricots

Young, waiting for the draft to war,
I picked apricots with migrant workers.
I found their valley hot in bursting sun,
A brown bowl walled by hunching, bear-shaped hills.
They moved through heat in sunken resignation,
Their blackened, sun-baked faces
Cracked like plates into impassive stares.
Their ladders pointed high to trees in lines
So parallel their bodies vanished into leaves
And sky like lives condemned to climb invisibility.
Their ladder life turned me to verticals
After a lazy, horizontal youth. This height
Was like the hangman's swaying stance.
Perched high with men condemned to ladders
For a little money, I ate the fruit of pleasure
And saw it fall into the fury of the harvest.

JAMES SCHEVILL

Surface Fishing

I am a fisherman casting
On the charming lake at the charming hour
When the sun is newly set
Though the light is little diminished yet.
I make parabolas with my surface plug
That is meant to counterfeit a swimming frog.

I am pleased well enough
With light and things in the half sphere
I breathe in: the early nighthawk,
The closing lilies, the late flock
Of goldfinches I hear while "Pop!" and "Glug!"
Exclaims my frittery, fussing surface plug.

Yet why should I be constrained
To have, know, only those pretties
That live in up and across?
I tire of being so long at a loss
For what is down, under. My podgy plug
Works hard at being a succulent swimming frog.

I want the nervous splash
Of the dark-muscled power from below
Rising to take my lure.
I want to have it, to eat its pure
Strength. Shall I change, let some other enticement fall?
For nothing comes up, nothing comes up at all.

W. R. MOSES

Conducted Tour

Who knows who stands there, ghost,
Whose shadow on the stair? Hamlet,
Leaving his mother's chamber
Boldly? an angry gallant—but let

His mother speak. Oh no!

A gallant wind blows
About the uninhabited palace.
Where does Ophelia weep,
No queen to heed her, stream for solace?

II

Look, before you go,

You can see the glassy
Eyes at dawn, the king at dawn
Glare, when diamond dew,
Still glistening, lingers on the lawn.

The hall echoes to tourists'
Practical clatter, though;
Prepared for quick departure
Enormous busses wait below.

EMMA SWAN

Peach Tree in the Garden of an Empty House

No blustering winter storm could fell the peach tree,
But when the fruit grew ripe, a burdened bough
Sagged, and it needed only a faint breeze,
A blue-tit's weight, the swelling of a peach,
And the bough cracked. Five branches brushed the ground.
The bark, exposed, at first was soft and creamy,
Stained ocher in the center. Soon its whorls,
Losing their smell of fresh wood and pulped fruit,
Grew darker, coarser, crusted like a wound.
Marauding boys, scaling the crumbling wall,
Ripped a few juicy peaches, but the rest,
Green, yellow-tinged, suffused with a warm dye,
Some delicately stippled rose-and-peach,
Were pecked and pockmarked by the jabbering birds,
Or dropped and lay discolored, squelched and foul.
The house was old; new owners chopped the tree.
Its piled logs saved them half a ton of coal.

JOHN PRESS

The Glassblower

Now see the shaper breathe and blow
From scattered seeds of quartz and sand
The crystalline and perfect O
That shimmers back at his command
The heavenly fire, the seven-hued bow.

Fine as blown tulip-bubble, frail
As dream—a touch could shatter it
That prisons in its burning pale
The moment and the infinite
With strength of more than triple mail.

Break it: the fragments would suffice
For new compounding in the flare—
But such harmonious fire in ice,
Such music frozen on mid-air
He could not so quite capture twice.

GEOFFREY JOHNSON

Beginning to Squall

A buoy like a man in a red sou'wester
is up to the top of its boots in the water
leaning to warn a blue boat
that, bobbing and shrugging, is nodding "No,"

till a strong wave comes, and it shivers "Yes."
The white and the green boats are quibbling, too.
What is it they don't want to do?
The bay goes on bouncing anchor floats,

their colors tennis and tangerine.
Two ruffled gulls laughing are laughing gulls,
a finial pair on the gray pilings.
Now the boats are buttoning slickers on

which resemble little tents.
The buoy is jumping up and down
showing a black belt stenciled "1."
A yellow boat's last to lower sail

to wrap like a bandage around the boom.
Blades are sharpening in the water
that brightens while the sky goes duller.

MAY SWENSON

Fishing

The wind tears at the water where I fish.
Suddenly snouts bite. Arrows of flight.
And as the heat sinks back wornout,
My shadow streams to greet the night
That floods a land tattered and torn
Where ancient snow is twitching with lights.
I dream of strangers in distant streets
Glistening with silence
Where never blindness and the severed life,
Of factories filled with radiance, where motion's
Shuddering emphasis is calmed.
Furious haste of wings.
Lights are fading in the water.
I find the crumbling rim
Where all are watching a strange darkness
Pecking out the stars.

KEITH WRIGHT

Vacation Snapshot

(For Fred Staver)

Your letter, fat with snapshots, came today:
The boys playing ball, our wives with windy hair,
Bright sunburns breeding in the hazy spray,
Our flesh as the reflex of water, earth, and air.

In sharp words, a sign beyond the rocks
Demands that we must leave no fire; the paint
Is fresh, this season's surely, time mocks
Us only, the outline of your nearer face is faint.

I warm each awkward picture with my hand:
The lens was on infinity—no prize
For these, and yet, the camera never lies.

Because we made the scene, we understand:
The faces are blurred, the distant driftwood clear—
We shall burn it again, against the colder year.

MELVIN WALKER LA FOLLETTE

IN A LIGHTER VEIN

Query

What would it be
Like to enter
A day which was
An immense cube
Of colorless, un-
Flavored gelatin?

LUCIE MCKEE

A Summer Fable, from Montaigne

A man with nothing to do (to prove or verify)
But throw a grain of millet
Through a needle's eye,
In time grew so unerring he was able when
Implored to by anybody
To toss it through again,

At which the gentle people—they who are last to wince
At any witlessness—
Mentioned him to their prince.
The man, they cried, is a genius, deserving of reward.
Their eyes were moist and shining
As they advised their lord,

Who, bound to recognize how long a man must try
Before he can pass an object
Through a needle's eye,
And happy to commend the piety, time, and skill it
Took (and encourage him further),
Gave him a bushel of millet.

HELEN BEVINGTON

Eighteenth Century Lady

*Her head was full of feathers, flowers, jewels and gewgaws
and as high as Lady Archer's; her dress was trimmed with
beads, silver, Persian sashes and all sort of fancies; her face was
thin and fiery, and her whole manner spoke a lady all alive.*
                                                    FANNY BURNEY'S *Journal.*

Oh, she was a lady all alive!
She bedeviled the beaux
who would woo and wive;
she wore no sackcloth
and no ashes,
she wore beads
and Persian sashes.
She wore feathers
and fine fancies
going to routs
and plays and dances,
with gewgaws, whims
and silver dresses,
and pearls and curls
and twirls of tresses.
Her jewels shone
like midnight's marchers,
her hair built high
as Lady Archer's,
with brooches, wings
and wonders wiry.
Her witchy face
was fine and fiery.
Her hoop it nearly
spread an acre;
she was a credit
to her maker.

Her maker was pleased
he could contrive
such a lady,
a lady all alive.

ROSE O'NEILL

Daphne

The sun god came upon her in a day,
And not by chance, at the wood's edge, away
From other nymphs, where she was wont to lie,
Teasing with nakedness each shepherd eye;
And whether pique at her unlikeliness
Or beauty prompted him, we cannot guess.

But the next day a laurel stood, whose root
Rushed to the final print of a small foot—
Then wormed toward the forest's heart. Its limbs spread wide
To the same sun without which it must die.
It shaded lovers. Through the fields there trod
Laurel-crowned men whose pride tickled the god.

Could they have spoken, the lance-shaped, leathery
Leaves would have perhaps conveyed a virgin ennui.

DAVID GALLER

The Marionette

Explosive. Start out
With regular fireworks
Of motion—arms, legs,
Head-duckings—snuff out
Just as suddenly. Collapse.
Now they're up again.
They think they can drag me along.
Hey, I was never one of them,
They're all of them nasty
And just asking for a good hard one
And the trapdoor treatment.
Oof. Hey, cut it out!
Come on, let them have it!
Give it to them good!
There's something so great
About a punch in the face. . . .
If they think they're so wise. . . .
Give me a stick, somebody!
Watch it, here they come again!
Come on, pile in, guys!
Look out for the strings!
Now! get them now!
God, I feel like a new man today.

IRVING FELDMAN

Conversation Piece

It settles on the lot of us. My wife,
Long sad face gazing into the dark,
Redgrove's huge bald skull
Seized in a rigid hand, the art student
Asleep, head slewed aside, like Charles I
After the axe fell. And even Eamonn
Set, in his chair.

        I watch
These figures from a modern frieze, and say
"The silence of the television age."
Nobody stirs. And I can't penetrate
The chill sarcophagus surrounding them,
Can only sit, silently, into the night,
Watching it fall, like dust, on each of us.

PHILIP HOBSBAUM

Reluctances

It never occurred to the turtle that it should hurry,
the spiral weighted snail could hardly go,
and, among the species that were furry,
the sloth was also known for moving slow.

Mules could run if they wished but they liked to linger
and clop along with knobbed, unwilling knees.
Reluctances of man to lift a finger
in fellow help suggested that one of the least

of his best qualities was samaritan quickness,
and not because of a shape that dragged a shell
or traveled the slippery trees with three-toed thickness.
A nimbler ambler, alert enough to tell

right from wrong all right if he had a mind to,
he could easily turn, as swiftly as a pack,
on ones he thought none needed to be kind to.
Lack of pity, undoubtedly, kept him back,

and modicum of mercy, with the beasts.
It took him ages just to face the fact
the maze was fixed, he'd never reach the cheese
unless he learned a better way to act.

HAROLD WITT

The Hermit

The hermit, sick of scabby cities,
Runs to a rock with book and prayer
To meditate in empty air,
To contemplate the shining brook:
Crowds are around him everywhere,
Blacken the sky, poison the air,
Litter the rock, pollute the brook:
They read about his peace and prayer
And they have come to share.

RUTH SILCOCK

Of Natural Forces

*In any contest between the imagination and the will, the
imagination always wins.*

WILLIAM JAMES.

The magnet said: "I
do not call.
You are mistaken. Try
for self-control."

The filing thought: "If I but steeled
myself, I need not yield."

The magnet moved: straightway the
    filing went.
So much for will. So much for good
    intent.

ELIZABETH CHESLEY

The Magnet Is Mistaken

The magnet is mistaken. It does have power:
  To its magnetic field
The little filing, with such small control,
  Just has to yield.

The tiny filing, were it but the wiser,
  Should ponder this truth well:
Free will is his who knows that he must choose
  The inevitable.

LOUIS GINSBERG

Quasi-stellar Radio Sources

At its far limits, the universe is daft.
Out edgeward nothing is itself no more:
Stars are no longer fat scuts of gas
But clots of stuff uncertain
As eccentric maiden aunts.

These lights called quasi-stellar,
Anarchic, observe not the curfew
Of thermodynamics: they run on
After they have run down, or
Shine with a brighter fire
Than they have fuel for.

This is not right.
For if I must pay for jot with tittle
And am not to be both big and little,
How is it they
Can play
According to neither Hoyle
Nor Boyle?

                    HOWARD McCORD

Samisen

You look
Like a classic geisha:
Your wooden pegs
Are her hair-ornaments,
Your white soundbox
Her moon-white face,
Your long, slim shank
Her thin
Elegant neck, elongated
As she intones
Some sad romance.
You both have catgut voices.

JAMES KIRKUP

Her Powder Box

This powder-box might seem to be
A sign of Nancy's vanity:
Not so, say I, who understand
How exquisitely she is planned,
      At once to be
      Yet not to see
Herself the beauty of perfection,
      And still to show
      Yet not to know
Such beauty cannot need correction:
Nothing but innocence would dress
In dust, her native loveliness.

WILLIAM F. STEAD

Take Notice

I will legislate in this poem:

Because my girl has large feet,
Large feet are beautiful. Be it enacted and decreed
That from this day on
Beauty shall begin from size ten
—No, strike that out—size nine—
And esthetic judgment, under penalties subsequently provided,
Will found itself in perpetuity upon my ground:
Beyond any appeal or repeal.

To which, I affix my seal.

RALPH ROBIN

Conceit with Aunties, Urn and Puss

Beneath the thorn tree's spikey shade
    My aunts sip milk and marmalade.
Throughout the Gothick afternoon
    They dance beneath a sun-shamed moon.
Their cat, a beastly yellow thing,
    Is humming snatches from "The Ring"—
While milky ladies spin and turn
    Before a classic Grecian urn.
And no one thinks my aunts abnormal
    In that English garden formal.
For, gathering by the tulip tree
    They crane, so they may better see
The fluttering veil, the bombazine,
    The peau de soie, the crepe de Chine—
All moving languid as they turn
    Before the cat and formal urn.
Miaow, miaow, miaow, miaow—
    The thing is singing Verdi now.

MICHAEL T. LEECH

To a Dog Barking at Night

I know, baby: as you fear,
barking brings no one back.
But it's a noise in an empty world
and it helps to fill the dark.

FRANCIS MAGUIRE

A Sound in Cambridge, Mass.

Every late evening in the silence before sleep
there's a crisp latch
opening in the darkness, the creak of a door
and two sharp steps
out to a porch, a balcony, and a voice
calling two notes.
They're the first two notes of an opera,
an aria to a lost cat.
She sings them over and over like a bird,
a bob-o-link,
only I never can hear the words that she sings,
perhaps Sam-bo,
Plu-to, Ju-no, a trochee, ending in o,
she sings it
always the same, never higher or lower,
the same breathless
expectation, the same lyrical patience.
And her cat
on a fence, in a garden, leaping at shadows, chasing
a velvet moth,
hears his own personal two-note violin
and comes home.

RUTH WHITMAN

Country Words

I sang a canto in a canton,
Cunning-coo, O cuckoo cock,
In a canton of Belshazzar
To Belshazzar, putrid rock,
Pillar of a putrid people,
Underneath a willow there
I stood and sang and filled the air.

It was an old rebellious song,
An edge of song that never clears;
But if it did . . . If the cloud that hangs
Upon the heart and round the mind
Cleared from the north and in that height
The sun appeared and reddened great
Belshazzar's brow, O ruler, rude
With rubies then, attend me now.

What is it that my feeling seeks?
I know from all the things it touched
And left beside and left behind.
It wants the diamond pivot bright.
It wants Belshazzar reading right
The luminous pages on his knee,
Of being, more than birth or death.
It wants words virile with his breath.

WALLACE STEVENS

Flight

An ardent owl flew
From the blue
Above,
And lightly
Alighted
Beside
His love.
Affrighted,
She cried,
"Pray, what brings you here?"
He eyed
Her brightly
And sighed,
"My dear,
I came
To you
With a blameless aim—
To wit, to woo."

WILLIAM WALDEN

Verse, Violence, and the Vine

Over the heady wine,
Well-watered with good sense,
Come, sing the simple line
In calm irrelevance:

The fathers on the shelves
Surely approve our toasts,
Surely are here themselves,
Warm, amiable ghosts,

Glad to escape our new
Regenerate elect
Who take the social view
And zealously reject

The classic indignation,
The sullen clarity,
Of passions in their station,
Moved by propriety.

J. V. CUNNINGHAM

My Friend the Caterpillar

My friend the caterpillar,
Too dignified to squirm,
Takes perpendicular delight
    In being a worm.
With feet in measured order,
His dignity to cinch,
He measures every measure twice,
    Inch by inch.
And yet he does not dally
As lazy squirmers do,
For his is quite a sure advance,
    Defined by two.
He measures once in rising
And once as he descends,
And so his journey multiplies
    Before it ends.
In this gyration, pleasure
Surely must be found,
For half his travel is by air
    And half by ground;
And in this double measure's
Symmetrical aplomb
He must know better than can most
    The way he's come.

DAVID RUSSELL

Dinner at Eight

The New Frontier by candlelight
Dine with Madame X tonight.
Down the white cloth public faces
Take their place-card plotted places.

Heads of missions, heads of bureaus,
Pentagon and Senate heroes,
Pundits flattering their sources,
Seven lavish succulent courses.

Small talk lost in big talk boomers
Rises to a roar of rumors.
Dear Madame X, you're a success—
Each guest is drowning out each guest.

Stocks are up but Laos falters,
Discourse dipped in wine can't alter
What is lost is not a nation
But the art of conversation.

KATIE LOUCHHEIM

Roadside: Spleen

These three robust black-sheeted sybils,
old as sin, have yammered like the sea
ten minutes now, about ten yards from me.
If they won't split up, I'll rebel
and read my blurring book a bench away.
One's apoplectic indignation spurs
the two who bear it to improve on hers,
which fords the first to yet more vital rage.

Rage, rage, immobile and inveterate,
lost breath, limp fury, and what waste of heat
from what charred bodies: I must go: but wait—
climax is bearing in! They terminate
in laughter. I am a fool's fool. And yet
something just now re-whets one's blunted bent.
Oh how contrition cheats us of contempt!
I am two fools. Farewell, friends, and well met.

ARTHUR FREEMAN

Ditty

Heavy of heart and light of purse
    Makes this verse.

Yet loose of foot and tied of tongue
    More than I
In thicker hells and thinner skins
    Live and die.

Twisted in means, and strait in end
    Have no lung
To air such cries: and what is sorrow
    Being sung?

Heavy of heart and light of purse
    Is no curse.

WILLIAM GIBSON

Not Self-denial

Not self-denial,
But a paradoxical Puritan indulgence
Makes me eschew
Ripe fruit,
Seething spring,
Sun spawning summer,
Round sounds,
Warm water,
Lushness, lusciousness, largesse,
For joy of a hard bed.
A bare room,
An underfed body, a spare
Hound dog, thin wind, granite,
And the silent economical landscape
　　　of winter.

ELISE GIBBS

The Troubles of a Book

The trouble of a book is first to be
No thoughts to nobody,
Then to lie as long unwritten
As it will lie unread,
Then to build word for word an author
And occupy his head
Until the head declares vacancy
To make full publication
Of running empty.

The trouble of a book is secondly
To keep awake and ready
And listening like an innkeeper,
Wishing, not wishing for a guest,
Torn between hope of no rest
And hope of rest.
Uncertainly the pages doze
And blink open to passing fingers
With landlord smile, then close.

The trouble of a book is thirdly
To speak its sermon, then look the other way,
Arouse commotion in the margin,
Where tongue meets the eye,
But claim no experience of panic,
No complicity in the outcry.
The ordeal of a book is to give no hint
Of ordeal, to be flat and witless
Of the upright sense of print.

The trouble of a book is chiefly
To be nothing but book outwardly;
To wear binding like binding,
Bury itself in book-death,
Yet to feel all but book;
To breathe live words, yet with the breath
Of letters; to address liveliness
In reading eyes, be answered with
Letters and bookishness.

LAURA RIDING*

* EDITOR'S NOTE: Since she renounced poetry, long ago, Miss Riding does not permit her poems to be reprinted without a statement explaining the change in her view of poetry. She has set aside this condition, which the editor has not found it possible to meet, because of what she describes as his "good understanding of her position."

Ulysses Pondering

Ulysses' summer mind was wont to think
when Circe's comely magic cooled his Greeks—
whose chains of being, now being bestial,
link-locked their human souls to animals.

And so by Circe's leave found he might talk
these bawling beasts back into men who talk.
And thought and thought the words that he might use.
Spent days beside the sea, the sun his Muse.

His mind, tongue-tied however, failed to speak
beyond the sun before each day turned dark.
In time he came to choose a fish-shaped rock,
as heavy and as light as any thought,
propelled it seaward in a rainbow's arc,
and, musing, bade it on the water walk.

STANLEY PLUMLY

Centaur in the Groundlevel Apartment

The mythical centaur
in the groundlevel apartment
lures me at times
with his lyric voice
to visit. He is janitor,
supervisor of buildings,
the only job he could get.

He is full of stories
of gods and heroes,
nobody believes him,
not even his wife.
But his stories
have a poet's truth,
are meaningful lies.

I listen. On the steps
we sit, and his tail
brushes the flies gently.
The night is Grecian,
before calendar time.
When he finally goes inside,
his hooves go clop-clop, clop-clop.

ERIC PFEIFFER

· 337 ·

About the Grass

Each fall I put down
tons of stuff and seed,
and still come up
with dandelions instead.

I say I care for,
not about the grass,
but for all I do
I do I guess.

Then there's our doormat
sprouting Merion
as violently verdant
as it can

to say, for all I would
about the grass,
how coming or going
green gets us.

                    JAMES L. WEIL

For the Existentialists

Conscience is you and God.
All men relive old stories,
A Giant looms over Jack,
Sisyphus rolls the stone back,
Lear rages, Hamlet worries,
Prince Hal outgrows and fails his pal.

What creature has the last word
Dear professors of the absurd?

WINTHROP PALMER

Sentimental Monologue

Young man that once I was, come talk with me,
    Here where you sorrowed for so many a year;
Now, in my later wisdom, I could be
    Quite helpful to the man who sorrowed here.

JOHN HALL WHEELOCK

What Makes Life Interesting

Sweet Mary primping for the prom
Felt worldly wise and lush as Helen
  Waste me tenderly, sweet time
She dreamed she'd turn Penelope
And weave and ravel for her Harry
  Waste me tenderly
And Harry dreaming of a death
With Hector's fury, flight and battle
  Waste me tenderly
Smoothed down his hair and tucked his tie in
In the green mood of sweet Paris
  Oh waste me tenderly

MARION MONTGOMERY

For My Shakespeare Class

This shabby, pencil-annotated text
Holds human passion, glory, shame and woe
Beyond my pygmy paraphrase. Although
Not unaware, I find myself perplexed
And loath to tell how youthful lovers sorrowed;
Instead: "Remember, class, the plot is borrowed."

The words of dying Egypt leave you shaken?
So am I—and fearful to intrude
On exaltation with a platitude.
Be glad I never yet have undertaken
To dim those golden words with my alloy—
Instead: "The queen was acted by a boy."

"Observe the purpose of each couplet ending,
Compare first folio with later versions."
These barren academical assertions
Are all I offer for your comprehending.
For human passion, glory, shame and woe
I think you're sure to know, are sure to know!

VONNA HICKS ADRIAN

Robin and Man

The robin, biped, beaked, worm-prober,
Stands stanch and sober.
He never thinks perhaps he should be
A bud or ruby.
He thinks, in fact, eternally
The worm's a worm, and he is he.

But man, admitted to the elapsing
Cosmic collapsing
Of all things, cannot choose but wonder
If he is thunder,
Its hearer, or perhaps its god,
Or merely cogitating sod.

RALPH GORDON

INDEX OF TITLES

INDEX OF AUTHORS